Lab Coats and Lace

About WITS   www.witsireland.com

Women in Technology and Science (WITS) was inaugurated in November 1990 to actively promote women in technology and science in Ireland. Our patron is President of Ireland, Mary McAleese.

The association's current major project is Re-Enter, an all-Ireland initiative to support women returning to careers in science, engineering and technology, in association with the Open University and InterTradeIreland.

Other recent projects include *Getting the Balance Right in Irish Science* (a report to Government, 2005), the *A seat at the table: Talent Bank* (a directory listing over 150 qualified and experienced women willing to participate in public committees and consultations), and *Jobs for the Girls*, a 'role model' and careers project for girls studying science at second-level, in addition to regular events for members and the public.

WITS published the first volume of biographies of historic Irish women scientists and pioneers, *Stars, Shells and Bluebells*, in 1997 and, with the National Committee for Commemoratives Plaques in Science and Engineering, has been instrumental in erecting commemoratives plaques to many of these women.

Join WITS: See the form at the back of this book. Members come from a wide range of scientific, engineering and technological backgrounds including teachers, computer experts, technicians and journalists. WITS members range in age and experience from third level students to some of the country's most senior scientists and academics.

Corporate members   have included Forfás, Science Foundation Ireland, Department of Education and Science – Gender Equality, IBM, the Health & Safety Authority, TCD's WiSER initiative, Enterprise Ireland, Teagasc, Roche Ireland, Kerry Group, ESB, and the Food Safety Authority of Ireland.

About the editor

Mary Mulvihill is an award-winning science writer and broadcaster. She edited the companion volume, *Stars, Shells and Bluebells* (WITS 1997), and her own books include *Ingenious Ireland* (2002), the comprehensive guide to Irish scientific heritage, and *Drive like a Woman, Shop like a Man* (2009), a guide to green living.

Lab Coats and Lace

The lives and legacies of inspiring
Irish women scientists and pioneers

Edited by Mary Mulvihill

WITS

women in technology
and science

LAB COATS AND LACE
First published 2009
By WITS (Women in Technology & Science)
PO Box 3783
Dublin 4
www.witsireland.com

British Library Cataloguing in Publication Data.
A catalogue record for this book is available from the British Library.

Cover design, text design and typesetting by Anú Design, Tara
Printed in Ireland by Colourbooks Ltd, Baldoyle Industrial Estate, Dublin 13
The paper used in this book is manufactured under the Forest Stewardship Council

10 9 8 7 6 5 4 3 2 1

In memory of
Dr Máire Brück, 1925-2008

Acknowledgements

WITS gratefully acknowledges the support of the Department of Education & Science and seed funding from Discover Science & Engineering (DSE). We also thank the Institute of Physics in Ireland and Biotrin for supporting the astronomy and zoology chapters, respectively.

Sponsored by

the Department of Education and Science

IOP | Institute of Physics
In Ireland

Cover images, clockwise from the top, front: Kathleen Lonsdale images, courtesy The Irish Times and Royal Society; Veronica Conroy Burns, courtesy Geological Museum TCD; Alicia Boole Stott's polytopes; Lucy Boole; Kathleen Lynn, courtesy Royal College of Physicians of Ireland. **Back:** *Zalutschia humphriesiae*, drawing courtesy Declan Murray; Annie Maunder's long coronal ray, courtesy High Altitude Observatory, Boulder, Colorado; Sydney Mary Thompson's 'erratic' samples, courtesy Ulster Museum.

Contents

Preface

In 1997, WITS published *Stars, Shells and Bluebells*, a collection of biographies of some 15 Irish women from the 18th, 19th and early 20th centuries. These 'scientific grandmothers' included many amateurs, several naturalists, and just a few who were lucky to find professional employment, usually in State organisations such as the National Museum.

This long-planned companion volume brings us into the mid-20th century and the era of professional science. The women honoured here include several who rose to the highest possible positions, holding professorships, leading university departments, and winning international recognition for their work. Many of them fought not just social conventions but also institutionalised discrimination to make their way in the predominantly male world of science, technology and engineering. We salute their dogged determination and perseverance, and the fine example they set for us. We are indebted to them all, for they paved the way for the current generation of women scientists, making it possible for young women today to choose whatever subject and career they want.

Scientists, writers and historians have come together in this book to acknowledge the efforts of these pioneering forebears. I am indebted to the contributors who took the time to research their subject, and to write about them so passionately and well. Thanks are also due to the many individuals and institutions who kindly loaned us images, and to those who helped in the early stages by suggesting candidates for inclusion. I would personally like to thank the WITS project team of Anne MacLellan, Dr Clare O'Connor and Margaret Finlay, who helped to oversee the project from its start a number of years ago, also Stan Solomon and Tom Bogdan who generously proofread chapter 6, and Anú Design for their stylish contribution.

We were saddened to learn of the death in November 2008 of Dr Máire Brück, one of our stalwart authors, who also contributed to *Stars, Shells and Bluebells* and who was a great champion of that first volume. As possibly the first professional woman astronomer in Ireland, and certainly at Dunsink Observatory, she was something of a pioneer herself, and will be sadly missed. It is an honour to dedicate this volume in her memory.

WITS gratefully acknowledges the generous support of the Department of Education & Science, which has ensured that a copy of the book will be sent to every second-level school in the country, and seed funding from Discover Science & Engineering (DSE), without which this project could not have happened. We also thank the Institute of Physics in Ireland and Biotrin for their support of the astronomy and zoology chapters, respectively.

Mary Mulvihill, Editor,
January 2009

The Contributors

Dr Máire Brück began her career as an astronomer at Dunsink Observatory, Dublin, and subsequently spent over 20 years at the University of Edinburgh's Institute of Astronomy. The author of numerous papers on the history of astronomy, and especially of women astronomers, she wrote the biography, *Agnes Mary Clerke and the Rise of Astrophysics* (2002). Her final book, *Stars and Satellites: women in early astronomy in Britain and Ireland*, will be published posthumously by Springer in 2009.

Dr Peter Childs is a senior lecturer in chemistry at the University of Limerick, with interests in the problems of teaching and learning chemistry, the history of Irish chemistry, the seaweed industry and the relationship between science and faith. His work in promoting chemical education has earned him the BP Science Educator of the Year award, the Boyle Higgins Gold medal from ICI, and an HE Teaching Award from the Royal Society of Chemistry. A past president of the Irish Science Teachers' Association (ISTA) and the Institute of Chemistry of Ireland, he has worked in Ireland since 1978, and before that in the USA, Uganda and UK.

Dr Clara Cullen has researched the history of the Museum of Irish Industry (MII) and its significant role in the educational, cultural and social life of mid-Victorian Ireland. A professional librarian in the university libraries of UCD and Dublin City University, she returned to academic life to research the establishment of cultural institutions in 19th-century Ireland. She has several published and forthcoming articles on various aspects of the MII's history, and has presented papers at national and international conferences, including the 2007 Conference of the International Federation for Research in Women's History.

Dr Dervilla Donnelly is Emeritus Professor of organic chemistry, University College Dublin. Her research interest was in the area of neoflavonoids and the natural products in forest fungi especially in *Heterobasidion annosum and Armillaria* species and she published over 120 research papers. Through her interest in European science policy, she has published and contributed extensively and is currently a science adviser as a member of the Austrian Council. In 1989 she became President of the Royal Dublin Society, the first lady since 1731. She has supported and promoted science through her membership of the Royal Irish Academy, the Dublin Institute for Advanced Studies and the Royal Hibernian Academy.

Seán Duke is a science writer, a joint editor and co-founder of *Science Spin* (Ireland's science and discovery magazine) and a former student of zoology at UCD.

Dr Aileen Fyfe lectures in the history of science at the National University of Ireland, Galway. The author of *Science and Salvation: evangelicals and popular science publishing in Victorian Britain* (2004) and editor of *Science in the Marketplace: nineteenth-century sites and experiences* (2007), she is interested in the history of science communication and popularisation, and is currently researching the impact of steam-powered technologies on science publishing in the 19th century. She has previously published on 18th-century children's science books, and on the historical relations between science and religion.

Laura Kelly is a doctoral student at the National University of Ireland, Galway, researching the history of early women medical graduates in Ireland 1872–1922. For her masters' thesis, at the University of Glasgow, she examined Irish medical students at the university between 1859 and 1900.

Karlin Lillington is a writer and columnist on technology with *The Irish TImes*, and occasional broadcaster. She has also been a contributor to *The Guardian, London Times, New Scientist, Wired.com, The Scientist, Business 2.0, Salon.com, Red Herring, Industry Standard* and other publications. In 1969 as a small child she encountered her first computer, playing 'hangman' with the famed JOHNNIAC mainframe (named for computing pioneer John von Neumann) at the RAND Corporation in Santa Monica, California (she lost). She has an M Phil (Hons) and a PhD (1996) in Anglo-Irish Literature from Trinity College Dublin. She grew up in Silicon Valley and lives in Dublin.

Dr Des MacHale is Associate Professor of Mathematics at University College Cork. His interests range from making mathematics, puzzles and teasers accessible to young people and the general public, to the history of mathematics and research in algebra. He has written over a hundred research papers on mathematics and the teaching of mathematics; the first full-length biography of George Boole; *Comic Sections*, a collection of mathematical wit and humour; and numerous books of jokes and lateral thinking puzzles. He is a frequent contributor to RTE and BBC radio and television on both mathematics and humour and his most recent excursion has been into film studies with three books on John Ford's classic movie *The Quiet Man*.

Anne Mac Lellan is completing a PhD on the life and work of Dr Dorothy Stopford Price, at the Centre for the History of Medicine in Ireland, in UCD, funded by the Wellcome Trust Foundation. She is a fellow of the Academy of Medical Laboratory Sciences and formerly chief medical scientist, microbiology department, Coombe Women and Infants University Hospital, Dublin. Anne has an MA in journalism and was a staff journalist with *The Irish Times*.

Mary Mulvihill has worked as a science writer, broadcaster and media consultant for over 20 years. A frequent contributor to the *Irish Times* for many years, she edited *Technology Ireland* for ten years and has also written for *Nature* and *New Scientist* among other publications. Before all that, she was a research geneticist with the agricultural institute, An Foras Talúntais. Instrumental in establishing WITS in 1990, she has been a chairperson of WITS and of the Irish Science & Technology Journalists Association, and a member of the Irish Council for

Bioethics, the council of the Industrial Heritage Association of Ireland, and the RIA Committee for the History of Irish Science.

Éanna N í Lamhna is an environmental consultant, writer and broadcaster, and president of An Taisce (Ireland's National Trust) since 2004. She has degrees in botany and microbiology and a H.Dip. in Education from UCD, and for 14 years was head of the biological records centre in the environmental monitoring agency, An Foras Forbartha, until its abolition in 1988. Much of her current work is in environmental education, at primary, secondary and third-level. Her latest book is *Wild Dublin* (O'Brien Press, 2008), and she is a regular contributor to the RTE radio wildlife programme, Mooney Goes Wild.

Dr Claire O'Connell has a B.Sc. (Hons) in botany and a Ph.D. in cell biology, both from UCD. She has worked as a post-doctoral researcher in Scotland (on the physiology of fruit flies) and Australia (on the pathology of brain disease). In 1999 she left the laboratory to become a technical writer and later converted to freelance journalism to accommodate an expanding family. She is a frequent contributor to *The Irish Times* and *The Irish Examiner* among other publications and recently completed a Masters in Science Communication at Dublin City University. She lives in Dublin with her husband and two children.

Dr Patricia Phillips is a social and intellectual historian, whose work challenges stereotypical views. She has written on the history of women's scientific interests, a 17th-century female writer of science fiction, 17th-century women's journals, early efforts to improve the education of middle and upper-class women, the development of the concept of originality in pre-romantic Britain, and the first impact of Surrealism on the British Isles.

Dr Patrick Wyse Jackson is a senior lecturer in geology and a Fellow of Trinity College, Dublin, and is curator of the college's Geological Museum. A former president of the Dublin Naturalists' Field Club, and of the Irish Geological Association, he is a member of the International Commission for the History of Geological Sciences and chairs the Royal Irish Academy Committee for the History of Irish Science.

Foreword

Dr Aileen Fyfe, Department of History, NUI Galway

As a child of the later 20th century, I studied biology, chemistry and physics at school, and no one seemed at all surprised or worried when I went on to study natural sciences at university. Although I later moved into the history of science, I have women friends who are engineers, computer scientists, astronomers and geneticists. Contrast our experiences with those of the women in this volume, and you immediately appreciate how things have changed! Science and engineering remain among the many professions still dominated by men, but there is nothing now to stop a woman who wants to pursue those career paths. Women are today found throughout the sciences, investigating everything from cells and semi-conductors to radio telescopes and barrier reefs.

The essays in this volume paint an inspiring picture of the pioneering Irish women who sought to gain education and employment in science, from campaigner Anne Jellicoe (Chapter 2), to veterinarian Aleen Cust (Ch. 3), to crystallographer Kathleen Lonsdale (Ch. 12). We should be grateful to them, even as we are glad that we live in a different world from them. However, not all the women in this volume saw themselves as campaigners or pioneers. Some, like geologist Sydney Thompson (Ch. 4), pursued their love of scientific research without attempting to build a career for themselves. Such women remind us that in the past, science was not necessarily seen as a profession. In fact, for most of history, science was definitely *not* a profession, and nobody – man or woman – expected to be paid to devote their life to it. The implication of this is that we should not imagine that women have always – until very recently – been specifically discriminated against in science. During the 19th century, the ways in which science was organised and practised changed dramatically: governments started to fund scientific education and research, and the career of 'scientist' emerged. One of the (inadvertent) effects of these changes was to make it more difficult for women to engage in serious scientific activities – and this is why it was that, in the later 19th century, women were more likely to campaign actively to improve their educational and employment opportunities.

Almost all the women in this volume were born after the mid-19th century, and many of their stories tell of the struggle to gain a university education and to have a career in science. What I would like to do here is put those struggles into an historical context. As you read the essays, try to set them against the bigger picture of change, in science and in women's opportunities. In the 19th century, we find some women happily pursuing science as a scholarly recreation – just as some men had been doing for centuries – but we also find some women hoping to join the new generation of men making a career for themselves in science. By the 20th century, science had definitely become a profession and amateurs were squeezed out: the challenge for would-be women scientists was no longer about getting a scientific education, but about surviving and prospering in a male-dominated profession. Doing so with a husband and children was even more of a challenge, though some (Kathleen Lonsdale!) managed it impressively.

Science as philosophy

For most of recorded history, investigating and understanding the natural world was regarded as a philosophical undertaking. It might involve using tools or doing experiments, but the purpose was to understand how the world worked and, usually, to appreciate the power and wisdom of the god who created it. 'Natural philosophy' was a valuable study, but it did not seem to have many practical or economic consequences. It was something a learned scholar might be interested in, not the state-supported profession we know today. From the middle ages through to the 19th century, most scholars were men and, therefore, most of the people who investigated the natural world were also men.

The exclusion of women (and the working classes) was a by-product of attitudes

There is a veritable 'sea of bonnets' in the audience for Michael Faraday's Christmas lecture at the Royal Institution, London, 1856.

to education, for without an advanced education, who could be a scholar? Education is now regarded as a basic human right, regardless of gender, race or social class, but it was not always so. Ireland's system of 'national schools' providing elementary education to all was established only in 1841 – and that was three decades before the equivalent English system. When education was optional, and came at a price, parents had to decide whether it was worth it for their children. Most working-class parents saw little reason for their children to learn skills that would not help them to be better spinners, colliers or farm labourers. Some aristocratic parents, confident of their place in the world, equally saw little need to educate their children. It was those in-between – the gentry, merchants, doctors, lawyers and clergy who expected their sons to have a profession – who were most committed to education. But sons and daughters were educated differently: sons had to go out into the world and earn a respectable living, whereas daughters would become home-makers for their husbands or their elderly parents.

Men certainly started with an educational advantage, but a woman who succeeded in gaining some advanced education – thanks to a willing father, or through her own determination in young adult life – could engage in scholarship

Almost as many women as men attended this scientific 'conversazione' at the London Apothecaries' Hall. From the Illustrated London News*, 1855.*

if she so wished. It was easiest for those of high social rank, who had sufficient self-confidence and position to disregard any accusations of eccentricity or indelicacy. They could afford tutors and books, and their rank opened many doors that would otherwise be closed. In 1667, Margaret Cavendish, the Duchess of Newcastle (1623-73) became the first woman to attend a meeting of the Royal Society of London. She could not become a member of this scientific gentleman's club, but her rank and her known intellectual capabilities ensured that the members were willing to accommodate her. A century later, Emilie, the Marquise du Châtelet (1706-49), translated Newton's works into French, and submitted her own theories of heat to the French Academy of Sciences.

Women consuming science

During the 18th century, there was a growing recognition among the middle classes of the importance of educating girls for their future role as mothers and educators of the next generation. It may seem a round-about way of justifying education for girls, but it meant that girls in some families might now receive an education broadly similar to their brothers. And unlike their brothers, their adult life was likely to involve leisure time that could potentially be devoted to intellectual pursuits. (Remember, women of this social class had servants!)

By the late 18th and early 19th centuries, middle-class women were more likely than ever to be receiving a good education, and this enabled them to become active in the emerging public culture of science. Bonnets can be clearly seen attending scientific lectures at such venues as the Royal Institution in London, and publishers brought out books aimed at women, from Francesco Algarotti's *Newton explained for the use of the ladies* (English trans. 1739) to John Lindley's *Ladies Botany* (1834). Certain subjects were thought likely to appeal to women: botany, for instance, with its associations to flower-collecting and sketching. Yet women were interested in all the sciences, and nowhere is this clearer than in the many books written by women themselves. Jane Marcet became well-known for her *Conversations on Chemistry* (1806), while Irishwoman Agnes Clerke (who featured in *Stars, shells and bluebells*, WITS 1997), wrote a *Popular History of Astronomy* (1885). As audiences for public lectures, and buyers of books, mineral collections and sketching sets, women were very welcome in the sciences, and more women than ever were, it seems, involved in the sciences in the first half of the 19th century. But does an interest in what we might call 'popular science' translate into active scholarship?

Some women were inspired by books and lectures to become serious students of the sciences. As long as scholars of science continued to be amateurs, it was possible for women to participate in intellectual debates. The main requirements were a library or study, which was, after all, traditionally part of domestic space (for the middle classes). Charles Darwin famously did most of his scholarly work at home in Kent, and some women found they could do the same. Englishwoman Margaret Gatty, for instance, managed to be a busy clergyman's wife, rear 10 children, and become an expert on seaweeds. But then, as now, marital and maternal commitments often restricted the opportunities to pursue research, as Alicia Boole's life illustrates (Chapter 5).

Even if a woman became a serious student of botany, geology or chemistry, she faced certain problems if she had original discoveries or ideas to present, thanks to social conventions about women's roles. Much of the scientific communication then was oral: important discussions and debates happened at meetings of scientific societies, such as the Royal Irish Academy or the Dublin Statistical Society, or during private conversations among like-minded scholars. These gatherings were effectively gentlemen's clubs. The best a woman could hope for was to have a letter read out, or have a husband, brother or male friend attend on her behalf. All these issues became even more difficult for women once science became a profession.

Science as a profession

During the 19th century science ceased to be an abstract scholarly pursuit and became a career. Starting in France and the German lands, and later in Britain and Ireland, governments were persuaded to see a link between science and technology, and thus with the economy. They began funding scientific research and insisted on science being taught in schools and universities. Local government, private corporations and universities began to hire 'scientists'.[1] To most men engaged in the sciences, these developments were extremely welcome: it meant respect, social status, a source of income and a chance to make a scientific career rather than practising science in spare moments snatched from work as a surgeon or vicar.

The impact on women was very different. Turning science into a profession meant establishing a shared identity and code of practice and, most importantly, defining entry requirements to distinguish between members and non-members of this new elite group. By the end of the 1800s, a university education in the sciences, perhaps with some postgraduate university experience, had become the normal training for anyone wanting to be considered a scientific researcher. Since the universities were traditionally male-only, this new insistence on formal qualification was a more effective bar to women's participation in the sciences than the social conventions of an earlier age.[2] Being intelligent, curious, well-read and well-connected was no longer sufficient to allow anyone – man or woman – to join the nascent scientific community. And once science was regarded as a career, conservative thinkers deemed it even less acceptable for women. Women could study the natural world in their leisure time, but to forego their role as homemakers and have a career was another thing entirely. The struggles for women's access to higher education were particularly fraught because, while an arts degree could just about be regarded as the ultimate 'finishing' of a woman's education, a degree in a professional subject implied a determination to have a career. Irish pioneers such as veterinarian Aleen Cust and engineer Alice Perry (Ch. 3) had to overcome opposition to their career plans as much as their choice of subject. It was not until the 20th century that significant numbers of women began to work alongside men in the scientific professions. Even then, they rarely occupied senior positions, or received international honours. But by mid-20th century, women professors and heads of department were becoming more common: Carmel Humphries (Ch. 9), Phyllis Clinch (Ch. 10) and Eva Philbin (Ch. 11) were all in charge of science departments at UCD in the 1960s and Máirín de Valera in University College Galway.

As this volume shows, Irish women participated in the full spectrum of women's involvement in the sciences. For some, studying subjects like geology or botany was a serious recreation, intensely rewarding at a personal level but requiring little or no contribution to original research. If such women did make an original discovery, they were usually happy to follow conventions and communicate their news through a male intermediary. Later in the 19th century, some of these women were important organisers of field clubs and societies which helped other women (and men) to learn about the subjects they loved. But more of the women in this volume represent the new professional face of science. They are the ones who sought to take full part in the transformed science of the late 19th and 20th centuries, and who had to surmount all sorts of educational, social, legal and employment obstacles to do so. They were trying to do science the way women and men do science today, and their achievements deserve our admiration. But I would also like us to remember the less dramatic women, who may appear to have achieved less, but who should be appreciated for engaging with an older style of scientific practice, a way once highly valued though now extinct.

There were several women in this botany practical class at the Royal College of Science in Ireland. The RCSI, and the Museum of Irish Industry before it, did not discriminate against women students.
Image: courtesy, UCD Archives

'Laurels for fair as well as manly brows'

Women seeking a scientific education in mid-Victorian Ireland could attend many of the public lectures organised around the country, but only the Museum of Irish Industry, and its successor, the Royal College of Science for Ireland (later part of the science faculty at University College Dublin), allowed women to attend formal lecture courses and sit examinations. Who were these early women science students, and how did they get on?

by Dr Clara Cullen

The first volume of biographies of Irish women scientists, *Stars, Shells & Bluebells*,[1] honoured a selection of our 'scientific grandmothers' for the contributions they made to their field of scientific interest. Among them were a number of 19th-century ladies: the sisters Anne and Mary Ball, experts on flora and fauna; photographer and philanthropist Mary, countess of Rosse; Mary Ward, an early pioneer of the microscope; Margaret Lindsay Huggins, a pioneer astrophysicist; Ellen Hutchins, an expert on lichens; and the astronomy writer Agnes Mary Clerke. Most of these women had to acquire their scientific knowledge and expertise without formal training, although most came from aristocratic or professional backgrounds, were generally in "a materially privileged position and had the opportunity to see, through the activities of their male friends and relatives, how professional scientific life was lived".[2] Their own contributions to science were, for the most part, published anonymously or pseudonymously, and they frequently worked as contributors and illustrators to the publications of their male friends and colleagues, or in partnership with their husbands.

One could be forgiven for believing that these women's interest in science was extraordinary, yet this was not a new phenomenon in mid-Victorian Ireland. Although women were not allowed to register as students at Ireland's universities until 1880, by the middle of that century women were a familiar part of the audience at the lectures run by several Irish scientific and learned institutions – attendance being available to those who, or whose families, were members of the various learned societies. From early in the century the Royal Dublin Society (RDS, founded in 1731) had opened its scientific lectures to all and, in 1815, the society's chemistry lectures were so popular that stringent 'ticket only' regulations were enforced, with a number of places reserved for ladies. The Dublin Zoological Society (Dublin Zoo) from its foundation in 1830 admitted women as full members and they attended the regular scientific papers presented at the society. Trinity College Dublin (TCD) admitted the public to some lectures and by the 1860s women could attend all of them that were 'suitable for ladies'.

Interest in science was not confined to women in Dublin. In Belfast, for example, by 1836 many girls attended classes at the Belfast Academy (founded in 1796) and "many adults, both ladies and gentlemen, attended the Academy's Natural History Society meetings".[3] In Cork, a strong local scientific interest prompted the establishment in 1813 of the Royal Cork Institution, and in 1835 the institution's professor of chemistry could assure a government commission that: "The ladies of Cork have a great taste for scientific reading".[4]

For the less well off, local Mechanics' Institutes and similar societies, established throughout the country from the 1820s, offered the opportunity for self-help and improvement to many ordinary men and women who could afford the institutes' fees (usually around 10 shillings [64 cents] per year). From the 1840s, under the aegis of the RDS and later of a government Committee of Lectures, formal courses of lectures on scientific subjects were organised in several provincial towns, and women constituted an important part of the audience at these lectures. For many of these ladies, attendance may have been simply social, but for others, their attendance reflected a personal interest and a desire to learn. Many of these, both in Dublin and countrywide were not 'high profile' and their activities have been barely noted or recognised. Their studies were facilitated by an institution in Dublin, the Museum of Irish Industry (MII) which, in the period 1854 to 1867, offered courses of lectures, both 'popular' and advanced, on physics, chemistry, botany, zoology and geology that were available equally to men and women. Outside Dublin, during the same period, the museum was also active in organising and providing lecture courses on a range of scientific topics in Irish provincial towns.

'The ladies of Cork have a great taste for scientific reading'

The MII was established by the British government in 1845 to provide a show-case for the findings of the newly-established Irish Geological Survey. It was intended to be a national institution promoting the sciences and their practical application. A building at 51 St Stephen's Green (currently the headquarters of the Office of Public Works), was purchased to house the new museum; funding was provided to convert it to its new purpose; and a director, Sir Robert Kane, was appointed.

Robert John Kane (1809-90) was a Dubliner, second son of a prosperous manufacturer, and a Catholic (see also Panel: The first 'Flora of Ireland'). He was by training and education both a doctor and a scientist and a man whose work was a "combination of genius and industry".[5] When appointed director, Kane was 36, held two professorships (at the Apothecaries Hall and the RDS), and had written prolifically on a range of scientific subjects. He later became the first president of Queen's [University] College Cork (1849-73), president of the Royal Irish Academy (1877), and vice-chancellor of the Royal University

Sir Robert Kane: as director of the MII, he supported women's education. Image: courtesy UCD Library.

MUSEUM OF IRISH INDUSTRY.
STEPHENS GREEN
1857.

The Museum of Irish Industry, St Stephen's Green, Dublin, in 1857.

(1880), and was knighted in 1846. By 1845 his interests had moved from pure science to its industrial applications, and among his major works was the *Industrial Resources of Ireland* (1844). He was also committed to non-denominational education, especially as a means of promoting understanding among the various religious groups in Ireland, and working together to achieve national prosperity.

Kane wanted the MII to become the Irish centre for educational courses in science and its practical applications – in fact, to become Ireland's first industrial college. The museum collections were developed with this in mind and, similarly, the institution's laboratory provided a practical service to local and government authorities, a kind of early industrial research and standards laboratory. Kane was determined that the museum's science classes would be open to all: "no distinction of class, creed or opinion … so likewise there is no monopoly of sex".[6] In keeping with Kane's belief in popular education and, together with its sometimes reluctant partner the RDS, the museum offered lecture courses of a general and elementary nature on botany, chemistry, geology and the natural sciences, both by day and again in the evening "to provide those who are occupied during the day with the means of employing their leisure hours in the evening in learning more thoroughly the more practically useful branches of science".[7] These were free of charge, and they were attended by audiences of hundreds, both men and women.

These popular lectures also served as preparatory courses for the more detailed and technical 'systematic' courses for which a fee, usually two shillings and six-pence [15 cents], was charged. The fee was to encourage serious students, "to test the reality of the wish to learn on the part of those attending",[8] and those who attended these 'elevated' lectures were expected to have at least an elementary knowledge of the subject – although the chemistry professor, W.K. Sullivan, complained on occasion about the poor mathematical abilities of the chemistry students. Ambitious students had the opportunity to recoup their fees by entering for the end of session examinations and winning one of the prizes awarded for the best answers, which were publicly conferred at annual prize-givings in the presence of the Lord Lieutenant and "the very numerous audience of ladies and gentlemen who crowded the benches of the spacious Lecture-room".[9] Successful candidates received certificates, and prizes of £5, £2 and £1 were awarded to those who came top in the examinations.

Few records survive of the MII students and there are no registers of the students who attended courses in the museum, although some survive for the subsequent Royal College of Science for Ireland (RCSI). It is impossible to say what per-centage of the student body were women but, given that about 15% of the successful examination candidates were women, we can assume that they attended in significant numbers. It is from the records of these successful examination candidates that we know of the women who participated in lectures, competed in the examinations and won either prizes or, in the latter years, medals awarded by the Department of Science and Art in London. From 1854-67, when the MII offered formal courses, women were part of the student body, attended lectures, competed in the examinations, and were what one Lord Lieutenant was pleased to term "ladies who entered the list as competitors and indicated the genius of their sex by carrying off the highest prizes".[10]

At the MII's first prize-giving, on May 28th, 1856, the *Freeman's Journal* reported: "Among the successful competitors were several ladies, whose proficiency was the theme of general admiration" and when the first of these ladies, Frances Elizabeth Armstrong, daughter of a Dublin builder, came forward to receive her

The first 'Flora of Ireland'

THE FIRST guide to Ireland's flowering plants was written in 1833 by a 22-year-old amateur botanist, Katherine Sophia Baily, yet went on to become a recommended botany text in Trinity College Dublin. A happy accident when the book was being printed, led to Katherine meeting Robert Kane, the man she would marry.

Katherine Baily (1811-86), was the only child of an English brewer and distiller Henry Baily, who moved his business to Ireland, and converted to Catholicism before marrying Brigid [O']Kelly. Katherine's mother died young and, after her father's remarriage, Katherine was reared by O'Kelly relations at Rochestown House, Dun Laoghaire. Her uncle Mathias O'Kelly, a member of the Dublin Zoological Society (Zoo), was a well-known natural historian,[19] and Katherine may have learned her botany from him, or from her father's brother, astronomer Francis Baily (1774-1844).

In *The Irish flora; comprising the flowering plants and ferns* (first published anonymously, with a second edition in 1846 with a slightly simpler title), Baily arranged the plants by category, giving the generic and common English names, a description of each, references to established sources, and locations for each entry (several of the localities being supplied by John White, of the Dublin Botanic Gardens[20]). Many species are recorded in Ireland for the first time in this work. In her preface – a critical review of everything written on Irish botany pre-1833 – Katherine wrote: "It is a surprise that Ireland has remained so long without any descriptive catalogue of its plants, worthy of notice ... While men of science have been occupied in investigating other countries not possessing half its richness". Sir David Moore, then curator of Dublin's Botanic Gardens, said this "portable book ... deserves notice as the first 'Flora of Ireland'".[21] 'Modest and accurate',[22] the volume became a textbook in TCD's botany department.[23]

Katherine subsequently contributed two articles on conifer growing in Ireland to *The Irish Farmer's and Gardener's Magazine*, revealing personal knowledge of these new plantations and the landowners,[24] and in 1836, she became the first woman elected a member of the Botanical Society of Edinburgh.[25] She was no mere text-book botanist and part of her herbarium, including specimens collected in the Swiss Alps before her marriage, was presented to Queen's College Cork during her husband's presidency there.[26]

Katherine met Robert Kane when her *Flora* and one of his scientific publications were being printed. According to her friend Lady Ferguson, the printers sent each author's proof to the other in error: "… the gentleman, much impressed by the excellence of the work mis-sent to him, called at the printers, obtained Miss Baily's name and address, and said that he would remedy their blunder himself by returning her proofs in person. The acquaintanceship thus commenced resulted in a congenial and happy marriage".[27]

After her marriage, Katherine devoted herself to her family and her

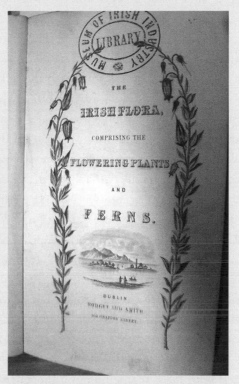

Title page of Katherine Baily's Flora of Ireland, *first published when she was 22.* Image: courtesy UCD Library.

gardens. However, in 1873 she signed the Countess of Meath's memorial to Gladstone asking that funds from the Disestablished Church be allocated to providing secondary schools for girls in Ireland in order to remove "the disabilities under which the women of Ireland labour in the matter of intermediate and higher education", and she surely supported or even inspired, her husband's views on women's access to education.[28] To Lady Ferguson Katherine was a faithful friend, while UCC historian, John A. Murphy, has described her as "the strong-minded Lady Kane".[29] She died in 1886 after a lingering illness and Sir Robert is said never to have recovered from his loss.

award, she was "loudly applauded". Another prize-winner, Halgena Hare, daughter of a Catholic schoolmaster, won first prize in Natural History, and was commended for her answering which was "remarkable for its excellence, general correctness, and number of answers". Halgena's sister, Miss T.S.A. Hare, was awarded a certificate in Natural History on the same occasion and a year later, Frances Hare joined her sisters as a student at the MII.

Robert Kane had always intended to "include the female portion of the community in educational arrangements" at the museum, and at this first prize-giving he certainly welcomed "the commencement that had been made ... in developing female talent in the pursuits of industry [which] could not but be productive of the most beneficial results".[11] However, even he must have been surprised by the numbers of women who attended and justifiably proud of their achievements. The first prize-giving set the pattern for the future. The earl of Carlisle, who as Lord Lieutenant attended several MII prize ceremonies and who was a supporter of Kane's ideas regarding technical education, also frequently referred to the successes of the women students. In 1859, he remarked how "The laurels that are to be gathered here are twined around fair as well as around manly brows".[12]

In 1867 the Museum of Irish Industry ceased to exist as a teaching institution and was incorporated into the new Royal College of Science for Ireland. The final examination results that year continued to reflect women's examination success, with three women among the 13 students awarded medals. The establishment of the new RCSI arose out of a controversy that erupted in 1862, as to whether the MII or the RDS should have overall responsibility for the provision of science education in Ireland. Three parliamentary commissions later, in 1867, an agreement was reached and the museum became the College of Science for Ireland, with Sir Robert Kane as its first dean. (It would eventually, in the 1920s, form part of the science faculty at University College Dublin.) The RCSI offered more formal scientific courses and was described at the time as "an institution which ... is more complete as a pure school of science than anything of the kind existing in Scotland or England".[13] It had other claims to farsightedness and innovation. In 1867-68 it was the first higher education college in Ireland or Britain to admit women as students to its courses, laboratories and examinations.

In November 1867, Matilda Coneys, a prize-winning student at the MII, wrote to the RCSI's academic council "requesting to know whether Pure Mathematics forms a distinct Course from Applied Mathematics, and whether she would be permitted to join it". On Kane's recommendation, it was agreed that: "Female students should be admitted to enter for the separate Courses of the Professors as heretofore to the Classes of the Irish Industrial Museum."[14] That year Matilda and four other women (including her sister, Zoe Leigh) registered for courses at the new college. Matilda justified Kane's support when she won the first prize in pure mathematics the following year. An early embargo by one of the professors against women attending courses 'given in the classroom' was lifted in 1874 and in that year three women registered for the physics course.

In 1867, the RCSI was the first higher education college in Ireland or Britain to admit women to courses, laboratories and exams

W. F. Barrett, in his short 1907 history of the college, describes how this happened: "In 1874, I think, application was made by the late Dean Stopford for the admission of his daughter to attend the Physics course. The approval of the Council and the Science and Art Department having been obtained, Miss Stopford [later known as the historian, Alice Stopford Green], Miss L. Digges La Touche (afterwards Principal of the Alexandra College), and Miss J. L'Estrange ... were the first ladies to enter; they joined the Physics course, and took a high place in the Sessional examination."[15] Although women were not eligible for RCSI scholarships until late in the 19th century, by the 1880s, after the Royal University of Ireland (RUI) was established and opened its examinations to both women and men candidates, up to one-sixth of the students on some courses were women. (The RUI, founded in 1880, granted its first degree to a woman, Letitia Anne Walkington, in 1882.) Many of these were pupils of the new women's colleges, notably Alexandra College (founded in 1866, see page 33), Dominican College, Eccles Street (founded 1882), Loreto College (founded 1893) in Dublin; Victoria College Belfast (founded in 1859); and St. Angela's in Cork.

Only some records of these students survive, yet we can put together a profile of the women students from surviving sources and contemporary newspapers and directories. We know that the students who attended the MII courses came from varying backgrounds. There was Miss Jane Anne [Jeannie] Leeper, daughter of the secretary of the Church Education Society. Halgena Hare and her sisters, whose father's address was the High School, 76 St Stephen's Green. Frances Elizabeth Armstrong, whose father was a builder, Adelina Rorke who ran a ladies academy, Eleanor Cope, a 'periodical dealer', and Katherine Elizabeth Egan of 11, Pembroke Quay, an address described as 'tenements' in the contemporary *Thom's Directory* of Dublin. Other students' addresses were registered to barristers and solicitors, to private schools, to widows, to merchants and farmers, clergymen, bank managers and a naval officer.

The majority were middle class; indeed, many of them were already teachers, either in the model and national schools or in private 'seminaries'. Certainly, some were "young women of the middle classes, living in reduced circumstances",[16] who were forced to earn their living. Others are typified by Miss Leeper who, like her mother before her, greatly resented that as a woman she was barred from higher education and attended the MII courses as her only option for extending her knowledge.

The museum's determined 'interdenominational' stand means that we can only guess about these women's religious backgrounds, We know that there were Catholics, and the daughters of Presbyterian and Methodist ministers, Church of Ireland clergymen, and Quakers – the latter exemplified by the five Peet sisters, who swept the boards in provincial examinations in Waterford on zoology and chemistry. The numbers of sisters listed among the prize-winners is also note-worthy. In addition to the Hares, there were Hester and Harriet Harman, Zoe and Matilda Coneys, Gertrude and Mary L. Hayes, and Clara and Gretta Strich. This trend continued in the RCSI and clearly reflects some liberal families and/or some strong-minded daughters and sisters, among them Camilla and Jane L'Estrange, the daughters of Sir George Burdett L'Estrange of Moystown, Co Offaly, who attended the science courses in St Stephen's Green.

Tracing the stories of the women who attended the MII is frustrating. They are, for various reasons, elusive. Consider, for example, this single letter in the files of the Natural History Museum in Dublin from the secretary of the Royal Irish Academy:

> *"Do you know anybody who wants a visiting governess—I have two in view who are invaluable. They took all the premiums at Sir R. Kane's in Botany, Chemistry, &c, &c. They are well up in French & that sort of thing.*

They can teach the young … how to shoot, or … to contend for honours in T. C. D. In fact if they were boys, instead of girls, they might stand for fellowships or cadetships or any other sort of ships … you will benefit three parties by doing what I ask."[17]

Sadly, no names are mentioned and there is no further correspondence. Other students make brief appearances elsewhere. Zoe Leigh Coneys was interested in women's suffrage and was a signatory to the first petition to the parliament at Westminster for women's suffrage in 1866. The Harman sisters were employed from time to time at the MII, drawing diagrams to illustrate lectures and making a reasonable living; in 1901 they were earning a living in London by their painting and drawing. Jeannie Leeper devoted the rest of her life to taking care of her parents and trying to earn an uncertain living by her writings. She never married and her brother in Melbourne, Australia, supported her, guaranteeing her £60 a year for life.

The sisters Jane (left) and Camilla L'Estrange, who both studied science at the RCSI. Images: courtesy, the Coffey family.

Jeannie Leeper typified the corpus of women students who, a few years later, benefited from the establishment of Alexandra College and similar educational institutions. After her death in 1921 her family described her as being "extraordinarily clever and if only she had been born in this generation, would have been really happy working for exams and honours".[18] As for the two L'Estrange sisters: Camilla never married and, apart from an unsuccessful attempt to become a 'lady supervisor' at Alexandra College, spent the rest of her life, according to her family, writing letters and visiting relations. Jane, wanting to do something useful with her life, founded the Dublin Workingman's Club. Through her work there she met and married the archaeologist George Coffey, and their home at Harcourt Terrace, Dublin, was a meeting place for many Irish nationalists in the period before 1916.

The next generation of women was more fortunate than Jeannie Leeper. Initiatives taken by education pioneers such as Mrs Anne Jellicoe (see Chapter 2) and Margaret Byers in the 1860s, the inclusion of girls in the Intermediate Education (Ireland) Act in 1878, and women's admission to the RUI degree examination after 1880 began a new era of educational opportunity for women. The first women graduates of the Royal University (the 'Nine Graces') included at least three women who had been students of the Royal College of Science for Ireland: Isabella Mulvany, Alice Oldham and Eliza Wilkins.

In mid-19th-century Ireland, both in Dublin and the provinces, there were significant numbers of women who attended courses of scientific lectures in furtherance of their interests and careers. Women such as the five Peet sisters in Waterford, Halgena and Frances Anne Hare, Zoe and Matilda Coneys and the Harman sisters, were representative of the many women, mostly unknown, who had acquired sufficient scientific knowledge and skills to participate in lecture courses on advanced scientific subjects, had enough self-confidence to compete on an equal footing with men in the examinations, and frequently took the prizes in the Museum of Irish Industry, an institution that was a pioneer among Irish educational institutions and provided equal access to all in scientific education.

Associated places

51–52 St Stephen's Green, Dublin; now the Office of Public Works.

Government Buildings, Merrion Street, Dublin: purpose-built for the Royal College of Science for Ireland, when it moved from St Stephen's Green in 1911; now the offices of the Department of the Taoiseach.

Portrait of Mrs Anne Jellicoe
held by Alexandra College.
Image courtesy, Alexandra College.

'The Glorious Privilege'

Mrs Anne Jellicoe (1823-80) believed that a woman's real emancipation lay in her right to work and consequent financial independence. A Quaker philanthropist and social campaigner, she established a range of initiatives to this end, notably the first vocational training college for women in Ireland or Britain, and her significant legacy includes a secondary school for girls that survives to this day.

by Dr Patricia Phillips

In 1861, Dublin became the first city in Ireland, Britain or indeed Europe, to offer technical training to upper-class women. The Queen's Institute offered Irish women a vocational education, with 'training classes' for telegraph clerks, for instance, and 'commercial classes' on a range of subjects including lithography, and wood and metal engraving. The institute, which lasted 20 years, was the fore-runner for other similar institutions and is a fine example of women helping themselves in a practical way. The prime mover was Mrs Anne Jellicoe (1823-80), a social reform campaigner, philanthropist and educationalist who later founded the Governess Association of Ireland, and whose enduring legacy is Alexandra College, a Dublin secondary school for girls that continues today.

For Mrs Jellicoe, women who could choose to work have "within their reach that privilege of which men are so proud, but of which men ought not to possess the monopoly – the glorious privilege of being independent". Her life was devoted to making this privilege accessible to women. She made it her mission to equip them to live self-supporting lives by devising appropriate systems of education that would prepare women for the work place. She sought to improve conditions for the mass of working women: peasants, female factory workers and women prisoners. Ironically, it was her work for 'ladies', the least employable of all, that was the most revolutionary.

'A job and a career was the only road to true female emancipation'

The Victorians perfected the shibboleth of the 'Weaker Sex'. Of course, not all women came into this category: well over half the adult female population worked, and often at heavy manual jobs. Ignoring this inconvenient detail, 'Society' cherished an image of womanhood, delicate and fragile, at best in bedroom and drawing room, lovingly nurtured by male relatives. Anne Jellicoe was one of the activists to explode this myth. She gathered evidence that many women from this social class were often unsupported paupers on the brink of starvation, with neither the means nor the abilities to look after themselves. Paradoxically, it could be more difficult for a middle-class woman to find a job with a satisfactory wage than for a lower-class woman: class prejudices often prevented her from taking the sort of work that provided economic independence, and 'ladies' were usually unskilled and ignorant of the demands of the job market.

In mid-Victorian society, it was expected that a 'lady' would not 'overdo' education. It was sufficient to struggle with the rudiments of French, a little music and, perhaps, some drawing, supplemented by hours of needlework. Even reading novels was suspect. 'Blue-stocking' inclinations debarred a girl from success in the marriage market, while rigid, social conventions excluded any overt discussion of money or, worse, ways in which it might be earned. Anne Jellicoe abhorred this travesty of education, the 'straining after' vacuous and useless accomplishments. She proposed a revolutionary solution: a technical and vocational training that would make earning a living a viable, even attractive alternative. And she went further. In founding the first technical college anywhere in Britain or Ireland for down–and–out 'ladies' she was unique. Her efforts to combat the deficient education of ladies were realised most successfully in the establishment of a college and school that offered women a complete and challenging education and allowed them to aim for the professional qualifications needed in the work place.

There were contemporaries (and a few before them) who thought that some women could, and should, aspire to the same intellectual pursuits as men. These reformers, notably Emily Davies, besieged the old universities, demanding admission to the Classical education that had long been the sole preserve of 'gentlemen'. But Anne Jellicoe's goal was not the 'dreaming spires' of Oxbridge, nor even the franchise for women. She wanted a job market open to all appropriately educated and skilled women. To her mind a job, a career – however humble, but with reasonable remuneration – was the only satisfactory road to true female emancipation. Although she was not alone in thinking along these lines, she was the first woman anywhere in the British Isles to put this principle into practice. Her work in Dublin was held up as an example to women in the rest of the kingdom.

Anne Jellicoe was born a Quaker. At the time, there were few members of the Society of Friends in Ireland, but their acumen and enterprise ensured that they made up a significant segment of the wealthy middle-class. The Quakers were in 'trade'.[1] They were famously egalitarian, disdained the established social hierarchies and had no aspiration to upward social mobility. They combined committed philanthropic beliefs with a lively interest in making money.[2] All of which helps explain Anne's inclinations: she believed in the enfranchising power of education; she had business and trade in her blood; and a knack for persuading the social and intellectual elites to support her projects.

Anne's parents lived in Mountmellick, Co Laois (then Queen's County). Known in the 19th century as 'the Quaker town', it boasted significant cotton and linen industries.[3] Mountmellick also had an impressive cluster of schools ranging from pathetic bothies where the poor learned their bible by rote, to well-equipped private schools for the wealthy.[4] William Mullin, Anne's father, was a product of this superior education and, as a young man, opened a school in Mountmellick for the sons of Quaker businessmen. The fees were high but the students were housed in modern buildings, studied the Classics as became men of their social status and, more unusually, also learnt natural history, book-keeping and business studies.[5] William died when Anne was three, leaving her, her brother John William (who later became a businessman), and her mother. There is no record of where the Mullin children were educated.

Anne was active in charitable work from an early stage, contemporary Ireland providing many opportunities for the philanthropic efforts of the better-off. Her acquaintance with Mountmellick teacher Johanna Carter was helpful. Mrs Carter ran a modest school for girls in a room in a thatched cottage. In 1824, about 15 girls attended, coming equally from the 'Established' and the Roman Catholic Churches. It seems that the only form of school work was reading the Scriptures – the Authorised Version – but Mrs Carter developed a further vocational training which may explain why so many Catholics attended: in the 1820s she 'invented' what became celebrated as "Mountmellick Embroidery", a *chic* product that found a ready market.[6] It was an invaluable example for young Anne Mullin, proving that work liberated a woman.

Soon after her marriage to John Jellicoe and their move to Clara, Anne opened an embroidery school (1850) and, in 1853, a school for lace crochet work.[7] Evidently she had some artistic skill for she designed many of the motifs that the women used in their work, basing her drawings on local plants.[8] However, aesthetics were beside the point. This was a money-making enterprise: Anne arranged for the women's work to be exported to Glasgow for sale, prices were set and the workers were paid. Anne Jellicoe had a good business head of which she was quietly proud, and through her efforts more than a hundred young women were gainfully employed.

But it was not enough for her that the women produced saleable goods – Anne wanted them to derive a further benefit from this training, and she encouraged them to develop a sense of self-worth and independence. Friends noted how she "laboured unwearingly [sic] amongst them to cultivate their minds and to teach them a just spirit of independence".[9] This was to be her life's mission. It may have been this aspect of her embroidery school that disturbed the local Catholic clergy. The parish priest, apparently at his bishop's insistence, entered the school one day and broke it up with his blackthorn.[10] In view of the dire conditions in the country then, his action seems perverse. Nevertheless, the school continued until 1856, presumably without the presence of the Catholic girls. Then in 1858 the Jellicoes moved again, this time to Harold's Cross in Dublin. There, Anne came into contact with some of the most zealous reformers of the time, found support for her own views and could extend her field of operations.

The 1840s were rightly noted by contemporaries as one of the darkest periods in Ireland's history. The depredations of the Famine and emigration fractured society and gave rise to social problems to which there were no obvious solutions. The Dublin Statistical Society (DSS) was established in 1847 to tackle these issues.[11] Its ideals were noble: it aspired to become a "living agency for good" and to work "towards the improvement of the institutions of our country".[12] The founders of this idealistic society were staunchly non-denominational and apolitical and, although none was a Quaker, chance brought the two groups together in a close alliance.

The DSS had a good relationship with another body, the National Association for the Promotion of Social Science (established in Birmingham in 1857), which held its 1861 annual meeting in Dublin. The association had a sizeable number of women members, many of whom attended the Dublin conference as delegates, all of them engaged in the question of women's education. The conference was a great success, kindling an enthusiasm to challenge outdated modes of thinking. The DSS acted forthwith and applied to the Royal Dublin Society, in whose premises they met, requesting that women be permitted to attend its meetings. The RDS declined this shocking request, and the DSS reaction was speedy: at an extraordinary general meeting, it voted to remove itself to the Dublin Friends' Institute, 35 Molesworth Street (where it remained for over 50 years) and there, in 1862, changed its rules to allow (among other things) "The Admission of Ladies as Associates".[13] Thus were the Quakers and the statisticians brought together, and thus did Anne Jellicoe became closely involved with the vanguard of reform. She found support and counsel and was able to draw into her own projects Dublin's best and most energetic minds.[14]

Influenced by these social scientists, Anne's philanthropic work took a new direction. William Neilson Hancock, whose own work was eventually the foundation of much legislation for the protection of children and young people, probably introduced her to the techniques of observation and research that she now adopted. His research methods surely helped her when she decided to investigate the conditions of Dublin's slums, prisons and factories. By the time the National Association for the Promotion of Social Science held its 1861 meeting in Dublin, Anne Jellicoe was sufficiently recognised in the field to be asked to contribute a paper. Her account, '*The Condition of Young Women employed in Manufactories in Dublin*', is an incisive and informative document "carefully prepared from personal observation and inquiry".[15]

'Jellicoe's study of working conditions in Dublin factories is incisive and informative'

Her paper collates data on wage levels, working conditions and possibilities for advancement in Dublin factories and sweatshops, and includes observations on the types of women worker in the various kinds of factories.[16] Anne also noted the sickening insecurity the workers endured: they could be fired at the end of any week without notice or wages in lieu – to face certain destitution. These women were helpless, with no means of their own to improve their conditions. And so Anne Jellicoe turned her fire on those pillars of society who objected to the education of the working classes. In fact, she told them, they had a moral duty toward their less fortunate citizens. At the very least some sort of provision should be made with regard to "such mental and physical training as will enable them more readily to adapt themselves to changes of employment and, at the same time, teach them their duties as responsible human beings".[17]

Her own suggestions were practical, well thought-out and in keeping with her now deeply-held philosophy. Infant schools and mothers' groups should be established. Adolescent girls must be encouraged into evening schools to improve their education, and these schools should be obliged to cater for their needs. Those unfortunate young women already married to feckless, drunken husbands, could be trained in housekeeping, advised on how to become "handy, thrifty and provident" and to look after their children. Above all, they must be counselled on how to earn and keep their wages. Penny Savings' Banks were the solution. Women should be encouraged to save what they could and be helped to protect these small, but vital, sums from demanding, improvident husbands. Finally, an employment registry should be established of the various jobs open to young women, and of the agencies that could offer assistance or refuge. This programme contained all the elements that Anne Jellicoe deemed necessary to preserving a woman's self respect and independence. She was not to change this, even when dealing with a different class of woman.

The 1861 meeting in Dublin highlighted for the Irish delegates the plight of many middle-class women. It had been an issue for some time in England: at the Social Science Association's inaugural meeting in Birmingham in 1857 the then general secretary, George Hastings, had questioned the supposed financial security of middle-class women. It was a topic that would recur. Over 300 women delegates attended the association's 1859 conference and, such was the interest, that a discussion was hastily convened in a corridor, for want of space, on "the industrial employment of women".

Some months earlier a pioneering body had constituted itself as the Society for Promoting the Employment of Women, on 7 July 1859. Its headquarters were at 19 Langham Place, London, and this address was soon a byword for the struggle for women's independence and liberation. The society's first steps were to assist the needy ladies of London by setting up a reading room and a meeting place, but also an employment or 'situations vacant' register, listing suitable jobs for women. This novel idea received wide publicity and, to the astonishment of the women at Langham Place, there was a deluge of applicants – all from the 'weaker sex'.[18] These fragile beings, it seemed, needed jobs to keep body and soul together.

Using data gathered from these jobseekers, the new society discovered several facts about the lives of middle-class women. They were often destitute, on the brink of starvation; they were willing to find any means of support, with one intriguing exception: none wanted to be a governess – hitherto the only acceptable refuge for the impoverished lady. For them, it was a condition on a par with slavery and universally loathed and feared.[19] However, the majority of applicants had neither education nor useful skills to offer an employer. The ladies of Langham Place decided to tackle this by persuading the women to acquire some training that would equip them for the workplace.

This should have been easy. A similar revolution in thinking had occurred recently in ideas about the acceptable education and career of gentlemen: a landless gentleman was no longer obliged to opt for a career in the army or the church, and was less likely to become a social pariah if he turned to business or trade, particularly if he was financially successful. However, even needy ladies were loathe to forgo their accomplishments for "semi–mechanical occupations". This was tantamount to losing caste. To overcome this sensibility, the ladies of

Langham Place persuaded sympathetic Duchesses and Ladies to register for the classes in secretarial and book-keeping skills, setting a fashion that lesser ladies might emulate with light hearts. Another incentive may well have been that, if a woman could not get work, the only viable alternative to certain starvation was emigration to the colonies in search of a husband.

In Ireland the problems were, if anything, more acute. The Famine had not only destroyed the peasantry, it had also reduced many of the gentry to destitution:

> *"The failure of the potato crop in two successive years carried in its train an almost unparalleled amount of suffering and starvation, and it was not until 1847 that the shortage of food began to bear its fruits of evil. As Mr Justice Lawson subsequently stated:– 'At that period estates were unsaleable (sic), properties were going to destruction, the entire of our country seemed as it were to be fast verging to the workhouse'."*[20]

Anne Jellicoe and some other like-minded women, notably Ada Barbara Corlett, decided to follow the Langham Place example and, on 19 August 1861, at the same time as the Social Science Association gathering in Dublin, at a meeting in the solicitor's room of the Four Courts, they agreed to form a Dublin branch of the Society for the Employment of Women. Anne Jellicoe had decided to narrow her target group. Henceforth, she would restrict her efforts to the welfare of destitute ladies and so, the newly formed Society for the Employment of Women announced that it would apply its "energies" to "the special case of gentlewomen".[21] The impact was astounding. Out of the Dublin population of about a quarter of a million, almost 500 women registered in the first couple of years. However, Anne Jellicoe faced the same problems as Langham Place, and the Irish ladies showed the same shortcomings as their English sisters:

> *"…there was the same deficiency of marketable skill, the same shiftless inaptitude for making their own way, the same dependence on a multitude of showy accomplishments, the same total absence, also, of that supreme command of one thing, which is sure to find its price in the market."*[22]

There was also the same "moral panic" among the ladies who registered.[23] They had nothing to offer but "grotesque expectations", yet clung to the trappings of

Commemorative plaque erected at 25, Molesworth Street, Dublin, formerly the Queen's Institute and now Buswell's Hotel. Image: Margaret Finlay

class and caste. Anne Jellicoe was profoundly irritated by their distaste for her own appreciation of a calling in 'Trade'. She could not sympathise with their horror of business and their feeling that exchanging money for labour was social suicide. She noted irascibly that these women thought it taboo to accept wages from those on a lower social rung; that they treated potential employers with "dignified patronage" and that they "took care to impress respect for their condescension in soliciting a salary, by declaring their ignorance of trade and hinting at a lofty contempt for traders".[24]

She would have none of this refined delicacy. She reprimanded these helpless and deluded unfortunates for failing to understand that "the faculty of earning" was in itself "a respectable gift". Merchants keen to help the nascent society informed the committee that "so universal was the ignorance of arithmetic among women, that in establishments in which departments existed where fashion compelled their employment, necessity forced the addition of a male clerk to overlook the bills".[25] And so, it was decided that the only way to come to grips with the situation was to set up what became the Queen's Institute.[26] In this, Anne Jellicoe achieved her ambition to educate women for jobs that would make them independent. There was to be no music, little French, none of the previously cherished 'accomplishments'. Instead, there was "business studies", and "secretarial skills" comprising writing, dictation (based on Anderson's *Mercantile Letters*), arithmetic and book-keeping. A class for teaching the sewing machine and related skills soon followed, because Anne Jellicoe knew from her work in the factories that there were jobs out there for women superintendents and overseers.

Other potential employers took an interest, including the prestigious British and Irish Magnetic Telegraph Company. It was attracted to the institute's 'graduates', not because of the social status of many of the committee but because, as Anne Jellicoe noted, they had discerned in the management – that is, herself – "the very pith and sinew of business". The Telegraph Company even supplied the necessary equipment and its principal engineer as a teacher. Many ladies found jobs with the company as telegraph clerks and were better paid than their English counterparts.

Mrs Jellicoe next wanted to "induce governesses to join the Institute", and to this end Latin was added to the prospectus. The plan was to educate these ladies to a high standard, award them certificates and enter their names on "the Situations Registry". They could then demand a salary commensurate with their qualifications.[27] In the event, and in order to found the Governess Association of Ireland, Anne Jellicoe had to take off in a new direction.

The 1860s were a flurry of activity and achievement for Anne Jellicoe. She had come up from the provinces, an anonymous wife of a man in trade. Yet within the decade she became a name in Dublin society; she had the ear of everyone from the Archbishop and titled heads, to the bosses of the business world; her work had been presented at meetings of the Association for the Promotion of Social Science; and she had spearheaded the founding of the Queen's Institute and persuaded Victoria to bestow her name on it. Finally, she would found the Governess Association of Ireland and establish Alexandra College, where she was to remain as superintendent until her death.

There were, however, darker clouds. On December 27 1862, at the height of Anne's drive to establish her project for the education and employment of women, John Jellicoe died. Using the scant evidence that exists, it seems that they were happily married, so one assumes that losing her husband would have been a great blow.[28] We know nothing of her sufferings and anxieties, all that remains is a record of unstinting commitment.

There were other undercurrents. Relations with Ada Barbara Corlett, the woman with whom she worked closely, had become strained. One reason may have been the haphazard fashion in which the institute classes were conducted. For whatever reason, co-operation between the two women ceased. When Mrs Jellicoe wanted to include governess training within the institute, Miss Corlett opposed it. However, by 1869, Anne's untiring efforts resulted in the founding of the Governess Association of Ireland, dedicated to the higher education of ladies who wished to become teachers. Eventually, students even obtained certificates from Dublin University (Trinity College, TCD) and studentships were offered to the less well-off. Mrs Jellicoe may also have begun to see the Queen's Institute as a stop-gap remedy for women's needs. As an obituary of her later recorded:

> *"In her labours here she found the work crippled by the utter want of mental discipline or habits of reasoning in those who sought to be benefited, and she said that to do good to women she must strike at the root of the evil and give them a sound basis of education as the first step in promoting their mental and social welfare."* [29]

This next initiative was to be her last, but also most enduring project. Using her powers of persuasion she again enlisted "men and women powerful from their intellectual qualities or social positions", and in 1866 Alexandra College for the Higher Education of Women opened its modest doors at 9 Kenilworth Square, Dublin. In an account of the college some years later, Mrs Jellicoe wrote that it offered an advanced education with classes in "Greek, Latin, Algebra, Geometry, Philosophy, Science of Harmony, Study of Language (Comparative), Natural Science with additional lectures in European languages and literature, English literature and History". Nowhere does she mention Sacred Scripture, although Alexandra was a Church of Ireland foundation, and scripture was certainly taught there. There were also advanced classes on Saturdays in TCD that regularly attracted well over 200 women, as well as gentlemen and university staff and undergraduates.

Yet, once again Anne Jellicoe discovered that these earnest female students needed a more thorough grounding than that offered by the desultory Victorian education, that "straining after the phantom of a finishing education". So, in 1873, she grafted on to the college a "carefully graduated system of secondary education".[30] Finding funds was a constant struggle. Mrs Jellicoe noted that both institutions were self-supporting, relying solely on student fees. With such limited resources it was difficult to provide a safe and healthy environment for the students or to permit more than a certain number to enrol.

Meanwhile, all contact with the Queen's Institute had ceased. Under Miss Corlett's management the institute lost its steely commitment to training women for work, and began to resemble other 'finishing' schools. The exigencies of class and caste also began to dilute the technical and business education that had been the vision of the founder. Support for the institute dwindled. Miss Corlett wrote an optimistic, if not very prescient, history of the institute, in which she outlined a splendid future of academic achievement, and claimed exclusive honour as its founder, making no reference to Anne Jellicoe.[31] Yet, not long afterwards the Queen's Institute closed. Almost immediately, a movement began to re-establish it along the original lines, to which end a meeting was convened on 2 November, 1882. Now it was Miss Corlett's turn to be ignored. The new committee declined to discuss or refer to the demise of the first institute. "It is a rather personal matter" was the cryptic comment of one member of the new committee.[32]

Anne Jellicoe did not live to see this, however: she died on 18 October 1880, at her brother's house in Birmingham.[33] Her body was returned to Ireland for burial at the Quaker burial ground, Rosenallis, Co Laois. The Church of Ireland Archbishop of Dublin, Dr Trench, one of her old friends and supporters, presided at a magnificent funeral in St. Ann's Church, and in his address accorded her the status of pioneer in the struggle for the equality of women's education:

> *"She could not but know that it had been given to her to trace out the first lines of a great work—that her name, for long years would be linked with a movement whose breadth and depth it is impossible to measure, or in thought to limit, and it will be only just that it should be so linked."*[34]

Yet, sadly, this link has weakened. Anne Jellicoe's name is not widely remembered for her revolutionary interpretation of women's education nor for her commitment to a woman's right to independence through work. Ironically, she is remembered, if at all, as a Victorian archetype: a woman whose educational notions were merely "to openly advocate and propagate dominant ideology", who conformed to the prevailing Victorian notions of decorum – in fact, as one who espoused little more than the "finishing school" model that she so abhorred.[35]

Certainly, she had to operate within the conventions of her own society, but it is a mistake to mis-construe these constraints. Certainly, she eschewed any political agitation on behalf of women's rights – but to avoid compromising her mission. The record of her achievements demands that she be recognised, above all, as "the apostle of employment as a means of salvation and elevation of women".[36]

Signature: courtesy, Alexandra College.

Acknowledgements

I would like to thank Aileen Ivory, Alexandra College Library; Tabitha Driver, assistant librarian, Library of the Religious Society of Friends, London; and Sue Killoran, Library Fellow, Harris Manchester College (Oxford). Fionnuala Cook rose to the occasion – as always.

Associated places

Mountmellick, and Rosenallis Burial Ground, Co Laois

25 Molesworth Street and 9 Kenilworth Square, Dublin

There is a commemorative plaque to Anne Jellicoe at 25 Molesworth St, now Buswell's Hotel.

Lilian Bland was a maverick: bland in name only, this martial arts practitioner was probably the first woman in the world to build and fly her own plane.
Image: courtesy, the Ulster Aviation Society

First in Their Field

Women who blazed a trail, paving the way for the next generation while often fighting institutionalised discrimination, included the first woman veterinarian in Ireland and Britain, Aleen Cust (1868-1937); the first woman engineering graduate, Alice Perry (1885-1969); and 'the flying feminist', a pioneering aviatrix who built her own plane, Lilian Bland (1878-1971).

by Dr Claire O'Connell

Had you lived in Edinburgh in the late 1890s you might have been puzzled to see a tall, striking young woman running through the streets late at night. That determined figure was veterinary student Aleen Cust, who staved off the chill of Scottish winter nights by sprinting outside until she was warm enough to sleep. Such grittiness served her well through the challenges of her student life and for the tumult of her later career as a vet in Co Roscommon, particularly as she had to practise unofficially until close to her retirement, when the authorities finally recognised her qualification. Yet Cust's lifetime saw many Irish-related firsts for women in science and technology, including her own acceptance into the veterinary profession, Ulsterwoman Lilian Bland's success in aviation, and Alice Perry from Galway becoming the first woman engineering graduate in Ireland and the UK. The changing attitudes that opened up third-level education for women during this period later spilled over into the workplace, allowing women to develop careers.

Miss Aleen Cust MRCVS: the first woman in Ireland or Britain admitted to the Royal College of Veterinary Surgeons. Image: courtesy, Veterinary Council of Ireland

Aleen Cust (1868-1937) was born in Co. Tipperary, where her father, Leopold, acted as a landowner's agent. A shadowy figure, he was unpopular with the locals, according to Aleen's biographer Connie M. Ford.[1] His position, however, meant that young Aleen and her brothers had the run of the Irish countryside. Little is known about Cust's early education, but Ford suggests that, as the only girl in the family, she may have been taught alongside her brothers. This, together with the rural setting, would have exposed Aleen to the natural sciences more than was common for a girl at that time.

Any idyllic childhood in the Irish countryside ended when her father died suddenly, and Aleen's mother Isobel moved her young family to England. When Aleen came of age she attempted nursing as a career, but it soon became obvious that she would prefer to tend to animals and, following a windfall inheritance on her brother's death, she went to study veterinary science at the New Veterinary College in Edinburgh in 1894. By now she had become somewhat estranged from her family, and the inheritance would stretch only so far, so Cust lived on one square meal a day and suffered the chilly Scottish winter with no heating. She also withstood the rough and tumble of the male-dominated veterinary faculty, where boisterous students would engage in 'muscle fights' during animal dissections, throwing chunks of discarded meat around the anatomy lab. It must have been daunting for a young woman to find herself even at the sidelines of these pitched battles, Ford surmises in Cust's biography. However, the young student maintained her composure, excelled at her coursework and, according to a classmate, eventually gained the respect of those who had initially jeered and considered her foolish to think of joining the profession.

Despite the glowing academic reputation, Cust was denied the right to qualify and practise as a vet. The Royal College of Veterinary Surgeons (RCVS) in Britain refused to let her sit the professional exams, although she was allowed to undertake coursework. According to Ford: "Probably the die-hards on the RCVS council hoped she would either die or get married within a few years, either of these fates being lethal to most careers for women, but to their subsequent discomfort she avoided both." So in 1900, she emerged fully trained yet could not call herself a vet in practice. She moved to Ireland and, with the blessing of the Edinburgh college's principal, obtained a post as assistant to a vet, William Byrne, in Athleague, Co Roscommon. Byrne's friends and colleagues were shocked when Cust arrived and turned out to be a woman. Despite the initial surprise, locals soon grew to admire Cust, who proved herself an able vet and an asset to the community. To assuage the local Catholic priest, Byrne said he had contracted her by correspondence and had not known she was female. Rumours were rife about the relationship between the dashing Byrne, a renowned ladies man, and his new associate, the tall and auburn-haired Cust. Both were unattached and attractive, notes Ford. There was also talk of a violent quarrel between them which culminated in Cust leaving, but the two remained friends and Byrne continued to support her career.

Byrne's friends and colleagues were shocked when Cust turned out to be a woman

Cust's romantic life was soon taken up with Bertram Widdington, the son of her former guardian in England, and after leaving Byrne's employment she spent much time with her new beau. They agreed to marry, but Cust's designs on a career were the undoing of their relationship. His parents believed that her commitment to veterinary practice (even if she could not call it such) would make her an unsuitable wife for their son, who was now in the British Army. The pain of the broken engagement may have kept Cust from ever wanting to marry, suggests Ford, and she seems to have avoided romantic entanglement for the remainder of her career.

Aleen Cust continued to build her unofficial standing in veterinary circles and in 1905 she was appointed veterinary inspector for animal diseases to Galway County Council, selected from a panel of three candidates (the other two being male) by a vote of 14 to 10. The uproar reverberated through the profession for months, according to Ford. The post was withdrawn and re-advertised, but Cust was reappointed as she was still the most suitable candidate.

Approval was by no means universal, but Cust had by now proven her merit in the field, particularly her ease of manner in rural life and (to the horror of many) her strength and skill at gelding horses. On a wider scale, attitudes towards women in the workplace were changing, notes Ford, and her Galway appointment re-opened public discussion on women in the veterinary profession.

Following William Byrne's sudden death in 1910, Cust succeeded to his practice in Athleague, Co Roscommon. She usually travelled to calls on horseback in response to callout telegrams from farmers, charging the wealthier clients while often giving money to poorer ones. She sustained herself on oatcakes and water-cress during the day and at seven o'clock would dress in 'a beautiful ballgown' and sit down to dinner, waited on by two servants. Cust's star continued to rise, both with her local clientele and with the professional bodies in Ireland and Britain, where she presented at conferences. The pressure was rising to let her sit the professional exams, but as 1914 approached, war took over and such plans had to be shelved.

Cust threw herself into the war effort and went to work in France. Horses were still central to fighting then and veterinary experience was needed to keep the working animals healthy. Little is known about her wartime work, possibly in a bacteriology laboratory but more probably dealing directly with horses. At the end of the war in 1918, she returned to Ireland aged 50 and in considerably poorer health. By now the climate was becoming more favourable generally for women in professions, and new equality laws meant that in 1919 the RCVS altered its regulations relating to discrimination against women. The way was now open to recognise women vets. In 1920 a determined young woman from Liverpool called Edith Knight had begun her studies and was on course to complete her professional exams in 1923. However, given Cust's career-long struggle against the machinery of the RCVS it would have been a "wry humiliation", according to Ford, if another had become the first officially recognised woman vet.

Cust applied to sit the exam despite a lengthy break from college. At the time many others were also asking for concessions, citing the recent war as the reason for their interrupted studies or careers. The examination board accepted her application and deemed that she need sit only the oral exam. And so on December 21st 1922, Aleen Cust became the first woman vet to receive her diploma in the UK or Ireland. The same week also saw the first women barrister, solicitor and architect, notes Ford.

Two years later Cust moved to England, aged 56 and in poor health. She eventually settled near Bramshaw and kept a number of animals including horses and dogs. She did not set up in practice yet continued to attend meetings and remained an enthusiastic supporter of women in veterinary science. In January 1937 she travelled to Jamaica and stayed with a friend and his family but suffered a heart attack shortly after her arrival. She recovered well but later that month she died suddenly, aged almost 69, having just tended to the family's dog. Ford notes that her hosts were shocked but realised it was as she would have wished: " ...working in her chosen profession and completing a satisfactory case". In 2007, this pioneering and determined woman was remembered when a commemorative plaque was erected at her former practice, Castlestrange House, Athleague, Co Roscommon, by Women in Technology and Science (WITS) and the National Committee for Commemoratives Plaques in Science and Engineering, in association with Veterinary Ireland. The plaque was unveiled, appropriately, by the Veterinary Ireland president, Ms Ciara Feeney MRCVS.

The flying feminist

Aviatrix Lilian Bland (1878-1971) spent only a few years building planes before moving on to other pursuits, but in that time she became the first woman in Ireland to build and fly an aircraft, and possibly the first woman in the world to build her own plane. The era of flight began in 1903 with the first controlled and sustained flight by the Wright brothers in North Carolina. This sparked a craze among enthusiasts for building aircraft, and Bland embraced the challenge. Born in Kent in 1878, she moved to Carnmoney near Belfast after her mother died, and was brought up by her father and aunt. Her family background was middle-class and relatively privileged – her grandfather was Dean of Belfast and her aunt was related to an Archdeacon.[2]

Lilian Bland was a maverick, and bland in name only. A sports journalist, photographer, expert markswoman and competent martial arts practitioner, she

Lilian Bland's Mayfly: *made from bamboo, spruce and assorted materials, it was the first biplane built in Ireland.* Image: courtesy, JM Bruce/GS Leslie Collection

wore breeches and smoked cigarettes, much to the chagrin of the Edwardian society around her. Michael McCaughan, keeper of transport at the Ulster Folk and Transport Museum at Cultra, Co Down, refers to Bland as 'the flying feminist' and says: "She was a hunting, shooting, fishing kind of woman. She wore dungarees and was able to work with machines." This unconventional woman developed an interest in flying machines and, when Louis Blériot flew across the English Channel in 1910, she was spurred into action to build her own plane from bamboo, spruce and other assorted materials. The resulting experimental glider – the *Mayfly*, the first biplane constructed in Ireland – passed its first test on Carnmoney Hill in 1910, where it became briefly airborne. The event was marked with a letter from Bland to the British magazine *Flight*, describing her glider's enthusiasm to take to the air:

> 'I had her out again today, wind of 18 m.p.h. My only difficulty is at present, to prevent her flying when I do not want her to. Today I had three men to assist me, two of them know nothing about it and she ran the rope through their hands and soared up 20 feet before anyone was prepared. Fortunately the third man and myself had hold of a long rope, which saved the situation;

in fact, we got the machine soaring beautifully for some time until a down-ward gust caught the elevators, which I had fastened, when she dived down and broke both skids, but did no other damage. It is quite a new sensation being charged by an aeroplane.'[3]

The next step was to add a 20 horse-power engine, which further tested the mettle of the plane's structure. Keeping the project going required lateral think-ing, and when a fuel tank failed to arrive in time for ground tests, Bland forged ahead by using her aunt's ear trumpet to pour petrol from a whiskey bottle into the system. The engine allowed the *Mayfly* to stay airborne over a distance of a quarter of a mile and at an altitude of about 30 feet, and marked Bland's acceptance into the aviation fraternity.

Bland had a local contemporary in Harry Ferguson from Dromore in Hillsborough, Co Down. A motorcycle and car salesman, Ferguson started build-ing his own aircraft aged 25, after visiting a flying show in Blackpool, England, in 1909. He made the first recorded powered Irish flight into a strong headwind later that year on his family's farm, and in 1910 became the first pilot to carry a passenger in Ireland.[4] McCaughan is impressed by how heroic Bland and Ferguson were as pioneers of flight, to sit perched in a small seat in their home-made, timber-framed aircraft, buffeted by the winds and rising into the air. Yet neither spent long in aviation. Ferguson's interest waned, no doubt hastened by an accident in 1910, but he later became famous for developing the Ferguson tractor.

Bland initially went into business as a plane builder, advertising her biplanes for £250 and gliders for £80, but her father, convinced that his daughter was lining herself up for serious injury, insisted that she leave aviation and bought her a car instead. She married a cousin and emigrated to Canada in 1912 where she is reported to have turned her hand to farming. In 1935 she crossed the Atlantic again and settled in Cornwall to pursue "gambling, painting and gardening".[5] She died there in 1971, aged 92.

Engineering her way

Another 'first' who remained for only a short time in her field of study was Alice Perry (1885-1969), the first woman engineering graduate in Ireland or Britain. Born in Galway in 1885, Alice Jacqueline Perry had something of a technical

Alice Perry on her graduation in 1906: the first woman engineering graduate in Ireland or Britain, she was county surveyor in west Galway for a while. Image: courtesy, NUI Galway

family background, according to Sidney Geraghty writing in the *Engineers Journal* in 1998.[6] Her uncle, John Perry, had invented the navigational gyroscope and her father, James, was County Surveyor (engineer) for west Galway and had founded the Galway Electric Light Company, the region's first public source of electric power. Schooled in Galway, Alice went on to study civil engineering at Queen's College Galway (now NUI Galway) and graduated with a first-class honours degree in 1906.

When her father died later that year, Perry was appointed temporarily as his successor to the post of County Surveyor for west Galway. It was a demanding job of inspecting structures and roads, and she had to journey around the rugged western region with less than salubrious transport. Yet she made her mark as an inspector, as reflected in the local newspaper: "She is the brilliant daughter of a worthy father ... the many and arduous duties of County Surveyor have never been better or more faithfully discharged than since they were taken over by Miss Perry.... and each and every member of the County Council has borne willing testimony to her outstanding ability..."[7] However, when her temporary position expired in April 1907, Perry could not be made permanent, being too young and inexperienced to qualify. She moved to London and was employed as a Lady Factory Inspector, enforcing laws relating to the conditions under which women worked. Of particular concern was their exposure to poisonous substances such as lead, mercury and asbestos.

Perry next moved to Glasgow and became interested in Christian Science, converting from Presbyterianism in 1915. She married Bob Shaw a year later, but he was killed at war in 1917. In his 1998 article, Geraghty suggests that the deaths of Perry's parents and husband may have turned her more deeply to religion. She retired from the factory inspectorate in 1921 and in 1923 she moved to Boston, USA, the home of Christian Science. She had planned to stay for only six months but she remained there, becoming a Christian Science healer in 1927 and working in religious publishing and writing poetry until her death in 1969.

Perry did not remain in civil engineering for long, but her graduation paved the way for other women to study engineering. Among them was Iris Cummins, who graduated from University College Cork (UCC) just before World War I. She in turn inspired a later graduate of civil engineering at UCC, Catherine Walshe, who in the 1980s became the first woman Fellow of the Institution of Engineers of Ireland (now Engineers Ireland).

The 'marriage bar'

DURING much of the 20th century, married women were barred from public sector jobs. For many educated women this bar thwarted their scientific and technical careers in the civil service or as teachers. The bar arose in many countries during high unemployment in the 1930s. The aim was to reserve employment for the traditional (male) 'bread-winner'; the bar did not apply to a woman who was widowed, and some women returned to their job after their husband died. In 1958 the bar was lifted in Ireland for primary teachers because of a shortage of teachers, but it remained for other State sector and secondary teaching posts.

In 1940, the marriage bar was challenged by a theoretical physicist Margaret McDonnell (née Gillen, 1906-89), who brought a landmark case against the Minister for Education after she was dismissed from her post at a teaching training college, where she had effectively held the position of a professor of science. McDonnell had married in 1936 and shortly afterwards was given three months' notice that her employment would terminate. Her case eventually went to the Supreme Court, which held that her notice period was inoperative and that she was entitled to six months' salary.[8] McDonnell, who was one of the first people to take a masters in mathematical physics at UCG, went on to work as a research assistant with Nobel physicist Erwin Schrödinger during his time with the Dublin Institute for Advanced Studies (DIAS) in the 1940s and '50s. She later taught science at second level, inspiring another generation of Irish women scientists.

In the late 1960s and early 1970s, Irish society saw many significant changes: free secondary education was introduced; the once-rural population became increasingly urban; and after decades of inward-looking policy, Ireland began developing closer ties with Europe.[9] The marriage bar was finally lifted in 1973, as Ireland joined the European Economic Community (now the EU). The number of married women in the labour force rose dramatically, from 8% in 1971, to 24% in 1988[10] and 54% – more than half the workforce – in 2007.[11]

Acknowledgement

The author thanks Pauric Dempsey, Royal Irish Academy; John Callanan, Engineers Ireland; Michael McCaughan, Ulster Folk &Transport Museum; Guy Warner and Ernie Cromie of the Ulster Aviation Society; and Catherine Walshe FIEI, for their help in researching this chapter.

*Sydney Mary Thompson
(Madame Christen) with her
geological hammer at Murlough Bay,
Co. Antrim in 1898.
Image: courtesy, Ulster Museum*

Erratics, Intrusions and Graptolites

A number of women have made significant contributions to the study of geology in Ireland, among them Sydney Mary Thompson (1847–1923) and Mary K. Andrews (1852–1914) who worked on glacial erratics; Doris Livesley Reynolds (1899–1985), a noted field geologist who studied the complexities of intrusive igneous rocks in the north of Ireland; and Veronica Conroy Burns (1914–98) who assembled an important collection of fossil graptolites.

by Dr Patrick N. Wyse Jackson

Geology has traditionally been associated with men, clambering over boulders and scaling rocky heights with a hammer in hand. Yet women have played significant roles in geological and naturalist societies in Ireland, and made important contributions to geological studies here.[1] Many of these women came from the north of Ireland, perhaps reflecting that region's rich and complex geological heritage. Contributions to geological studies prior to the 1920s were predominantly made by amateurs associated with the various field clubs around the country, and three of the women featured here fall into this category. Our fourth subject, Doris Reynolds, was employed as an assistant at Queen's University, Belfast (QUB) in the 1920s, but such university appointments of women were rare. Indeed, even today Ireland's geological community remains generally male-dominated, although in recent years the number of women taking geology degrees at university has grown significantly.

For most of the 20th century, however, few women held significant positions in the university or government sectors. The first women geologists were appointed to the Geological Survey of Ireland (GSI) in the late 1950s and the first woman lecturer in a geology department in Ireland in 1963. These women did not progress far up the promotional ladder and most moved on within a few years. In Trinity College, Dublin (TCD), even in the late 1970s there were some who opposed the progression of women students to the honours programme, but this opposition was resisted. By 2000, there were women geologists on the academic staff of all Irish universities and the numbers of women employed as geologists in the Geological Surveys of Ireland and Northern Ireland had increased.

Glacial erratics in the north of Ireland

In 1840, Louis Agassiz, a Swiss geologist, travelled through Britain and Ireland and announced, to the incredulity of many scientists, that he had found evidence of former glaciers throughout the countryside. The evidence included glacial erratics: in strict geological parlance these are large boulders or rock, that had been picked up by the ice and carried some distance and came to be deposited on top of a different rock-type when the ice sheets melted. The term 'erratic' was also applied to smaller fragments of exotic material caught up in sand and gravel deposited by the ice. While Agassiz's theory of former Ice Ages took some time to be generally accepted, by the 1870s many scientists had begun to map the distribution of erratics. This was in vogue at the time – among other things, it helped to reveal the direction and route taken by the long-vanished ice – so much so that the British Association for the Advancement of Science (BAAS) established a committee to report on the subject, and between 1874–1908 it even granted the considerable sum of £157-16s-6d to support this work.[2]

In Belfast during the 1890s, a group of amateur geologists became interested in the distribution of glacial erratics in the north of Ireland, keen to determine the direction of ice-flow in Ulster. They formed the Geological Section of the oldest field club in Ireland – the Belfast Naturalists' Field Club (BNFC), founded in 1863 and still on the go. Its secretary and leading light for many years was

Sydney Mary Thompson (1847-1923), who had a keen interest in geology and was aided in her labours by another woman, Mary K. Andrews (1852-1914).[3]

Thompson was born at Whitehouse, Co. Antrim, one of several children of James Thompson, a Belfast linen merchant, and a niece of the naturalist William Thompson. Following her schooling, and three years in Dresden, Germany, she enrolled at the Belfast Government School of Art in 1870 where she gained several prizes.[4] She later trained in South Kensington and subsequently joined two groups of artists on her return home: the Belfast Ramblers'

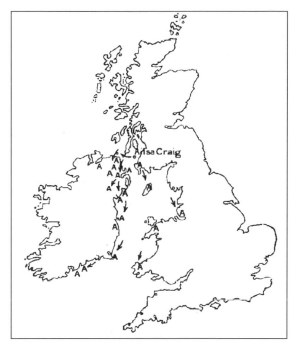

Figure 1. *Distribution of Ailsa Craig granite erratics in Ireland and Britain, deposited by the Irish Sea Glacier. Sydney Mary Thompson discovered the most westerly point in the north.* (From W.B. Wright, The Quarternary Ice Age, Macmillan, London (1914), p. 56)

Sketching Club and the Belfast Art Society, becoming patron of the latter from 1921. With her sister she shared a studio in their father's house at Macedon Point, north of Belfast. At the age of 53, Thompson married a Swiss artist Rodolphe Christen and was from then on styled 'Madame Christen'. Rodolphe was the seventh son of Melchior Christen and lived at St Imier, near Berne in Switzerland.[5] Following their marriage they travelled throughout continental Europe for two years before building their own house, which they called St Imier, in Ballater, Aberdeenshire, Scotland. Unfortunately the couple enjoyed a brief marriage: Rodolphe died at home on 7th September 1906 aged only 47. Madame Christen herself died of heart-failure in Landudno, on the north coast of Wales on 16th July 1923.

Mary K. Andrews was born in Belfast, one of six children and four daughters of Thomas Andrews (1813-1885), QUB's first professor of chemisty and its first vice-president,[6] and his wife Jane (née Hardie). His major research was on

The erratic samples collected by Sydney Mary Thompson and her colleagues in the Belfast Naturalists' Field Club are now in the Ulster Museum. Image: courtesy, Ulster Museum

ozone and other gases and he had shown how they could be liquified, a state that is exploited in modern refrigerators. For many years until her death Mary, his unmarried daughter, lived close to the university at 12, College Gardens. Little is known of her education, and nothing of why she developed her geological interests. She may have had a university education in geology, but even if she was self-taught she was confident enough to attend the Congress Auxiliary of the World's Columbian Exposition which took place in Chicago in August 1893.

This event, also known as the Chicago World's Fair, was part of the celebrations to mark the 400th anniversary of Christopher Columbus's discovery of the New World. There, with other women from North America and Britain she contributed to the Woman's Section of the Congress on Geology[7] – the men met separately for their own convention.[8] Short sessions were held throughout the week: Andrews gave a paper on 'Physical Geology', while Agnes Crane of Brighton read one on 'The evolution of the Brachiopoda', and Jane Donald of Carlisle spoke on 'Paleontology'. Donald was a noted expert on fossil gastropods (the class of animals that today includes snails and whelks) from the Palaeozoic era, some 540–250 million years ago.[9]

We can get a sense of Mary Andrews's character from the fact that, when she later became interested in the metamorphosed chalk found at Scawt Hill north of Larne,[10] she did not publish her findings. Instead, she freely gave her rock specimens and observations to George Gough of Cirencester who utilised them in his assessment of the chalk and its metamorphism.[11] That a woman would allow a man to publish her findings is typical for the time.

Sydney Mary Thompson was, from an early age, a keen student of glacial features. In 1894 she was elected a member of the Glacialists' Association and she also joined the Geologists' Association (both associations aspired to be international, but drew their membership primarily from Britain and less so from Ireland and continental Europe). Thompson quickly began to make her mark as a geologist. In July 1895 she organised a visit to the region by the Geologists' Association, during which they enjoyed her hospitality with a visit to her father's house.[12] She and Miss Andrews and a few other BNFC members were inspired by Percy Fry Kendall, a leading member of the Glacialists' Association and professor of geology at the University of Leeds, who had done much to promote the study of erratics. They formed a geological committee which was part of the larger field club and between 1893 and 1899 they mapped, named and collected samples of these exotic blocks of rock, with a view to determining the direction of ice-flow in Ulster. Their results were written up by Thompson, as secretary of the geology committee, and published in the *Proceedings* of the BNFC, and they also contributed their findings to the BAAS committee.

Mary Creese, who has published extensive research on women scientists of this period, has noted that Thompson's major find was a piece of Ailsa Craig microgranite at Moys, inland from Limavady, Co. Derry, which demonstrated the most westerly extent of the Irish Sea Glacier, during the last Ice Age some 198,000 years ago.[13] This distinctive granite, from a small island on Scotland's southwest coast, contains tiny flecks of a blue-coloured mineral, rebeckite. Small pieces of the rock were carried by the Irish Sea Glacier southwards and deposited with glacial sediments along the east coast of Ireland (Figure 1), and its presence allows geologists to trace the flow of this long-melted glacier. Today, the Belfast group's collection of erratics is in the Ulster Museum, where the small samples are wrapped in brown paper tied neatly with pink ribbon.[14]

In 1901, Mary Andrews published an important paper on fossil shells and foraminifera (microscopic shells from tiny, single-celled marine animals) collected from glacial sands at Moel Tryfaen in north Wales. The importance of this site is that it is high above sea level and revealed how ice can deposit marine shells at high elevations. Andrews recognised the presence of 12 species, all told, and her findings were utilised by an eminent micro-palaeontologist, Joseph Wright, in a report to the BAAS.[15]

Another 'British Association' initiative was collecting photographs of geological features in Britain and Ireland, and several Irish photographers contributed prints. By the time the association gathered in Dublin for its 1908 annual meeting, the collection contained 669 images taken in Ireland. The bulk of these were scenes in Co. Antrim (287 images), and the majority of the Irish images had been taken by Robert John Welch, a noted Belfast photographer.[16] Others were supplied by Prof. Grenville Cole of Dublin,[17] Prof. Sidney Reynolds of Bristol, J. St. J. Phillips and W. Grey of Belfast, and by Mary K. Andrews. Andrews was an enthusiastic photographer of some ability, and she often assembled sets of Irish views for the annual BAAS meetings. Most of her photographs were taken in Ireland between 1895 and 1907, and they include a quarry at Templepatrick, Co. Antrim, in which a succession of chalk, rhyolite and basalt was exposed; Whitewell Quarry near Belfast where the chalk is cross-cut by a basalt dyke; and the rare orbicular granite at Mullaghderg, Co. Donegal.[18] Andrews also supplied photographs of geological features in Dorset. Many of the photographs of Irish geological features are now in the collections of the Ulster Museum. In 1898, W. W. Watts, secretary of the BAAS geological photographic committee, included a drawing from one of Andrews's photographs of a dyke cross-cutting Triassic sandstone in his popular textbook *Geology for Beginners*, which went to several editions.[19]

In addition to their reports on glacial phenomena, the Belfast ladies also published other geological papers (see: Notes and sources). Andrews wrote on dykes in Antrim and Down; Thompson published a short note on mussels and, in 1910, a biography of her late husband in which is reproduced his pencil drawing of her cutting their wedding cake whilst on a picnic. Appropriately, she is sheltering in the shadow of a large erratic.[20]

Igneous studies

Doris Livesley Reynolds (1899–1985) is now remembered by many geologists as the wife of the celebrated geologist Arthur Holmes, who devised the first absolute timescale for the age of the Earth by applying radiometric dating of rocks throughout the geological succession.[21] However, Doris was a geologist of considerable ability, which was recognised by her peers when she was awarded the Lyell Medal of the Geological Society of London in 1960. Although not born in Ireland, her parents had moved from Belfast to Manchester shortly before her birth, and she was on the staff of Queen's University, Belfast between 1921 and 1926. It was in the igneous regions of Ulster where she carried out her most important work, and as such she deserves inclusion in this volume.

Educated in Essex, Reynolds received her geological education under the redoubtable Catherine Raisin at Bedford

Doris Reynolds and Arthur Holmes in Ireland. Reynolds mapped several of the igneous formations in the north of Ireland. Image: courtesy, Cherry Lewis

College, a constituent college of the University of London that had been established for the education of women.[22] Doris gained first class honours and graduated with a B.A. in 1920 and was immediately employed at QUB by Arthur Dwerryhouse as his research assistant. Soon after she arrived he moved to Reading, but she remained as assistant to his successor, John Kaye Charlesworth, a glacial geologist. In 1926 she returned to Bedford College as lecturer in petrology, and received the degree of D.Sc. in 1927. In 1933 she was appointed by Arthur Holmes to a lecturership in Durham and in 1939 they married shortly after the death of his wife. Unease about this relationship permeated the university and Holmes and Reynolds moved to Edinburgh in 1943 when he was appointed

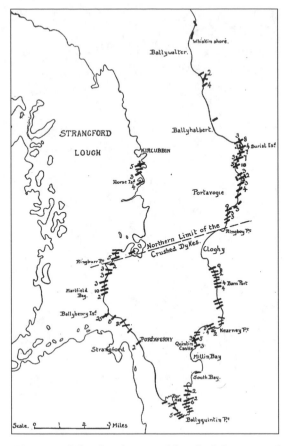

Figure 2. *The distribution of basalt dykes around the Ards Peninsula, Co. Down, as mapped by Doris Reynolds (from Reynolds (1931).*

to a Chair in geology.[23] On retirement they moved to the south of England and Doris died in 1985 having survived her husband by two decades.

Doris published a series of papers on the geology of the north of Ireland. One of her first featured the same Triassic sandstones photographed by Mary Andrews many years earlier. However, her papers on the igneous rocks brought her most acclaim. Among the first of these was a short article that featured some small vertical emplacements of basalt, called dykes, which she had mapped throughout the Ards Peninsula (Figure 2). Moving on to larger field areas she tackled the impressive igneous intrusions around Newry and Slieve Gullion, and in time she published a number of detailed geological papers and maps of the district. She also contributed to what became known as the 'granite controversy' during the 1930s and 1940s, when various geologists debated the nature and formation of granite. Reynolds also produced a plausible and now accepted account of the mechanism for the formation of rare sodium-rich rocks called albite, which she argued were formed during metamorphism through the introduction of hot fluids.

Doris Reynolds was a woman with huge energy and, it was said, she was strongly opinionated and feisty. She spent many years working on the geology of her parents' homeland, and contributed a large volume of published work (see: Notes and sources). Of the field geologists working in Ireland during the first half of the 20th century, I suggest that her contributions were among the most significant internationally.

Stars, graptolites, and museum collections

The Dublin Naturalists' Field Club was established in 1886 and over the years its strengths have largely been in the field of botany. Geology generally received less attention, but between the 1950s and 1970s two women associated with TCD did much to promote the subject amongst fellow club members. Barbara Miller (née Thompson), who had been a graduate student in geology, served as president of the club in 1965–'66 and led 24 geological excursions between 1957 and 1979, while Veronica Conroy Burns led 19 trips over 27 years until 1986.[24]

Veronica Conroy Burns was born at Calvinstown, Co. Kildare on 13th November 1914 and died in the Molyneux Home, Leeson Park, Dublin on 5th January 1998 aged 83.[25] Raised by foster parents in Dublin, she lived in a garden flat at 39 Pembroke Road in Ballsbridge, which remained her home for all but the last two years of her life. Largely self-educated, Veronica developed interests in astronomy, classical archaeology, natural history and geology. She worked for a period as an assistant at Armagh Observatory in the 1940s under its then director, Eric Lindsay, where among other duties she assembled meteorological records,[26] and she was a founder member in 1938 of the Irish Astronomical Society.[27] Later she worked in a photographic studio in Dublin. Her wartime Travel Permit Card,[28] issued on 23rd October 1944 to allow her to travel between the Republic of Ireland and Britain, describes her as a 'Junior Observatory Assistant'. This she used to travel to work as a laboratory assistant first with Goodman's Industries, Wembley, and later with GEC Research Laboratory, East Lane Wembley.

In 1964 she was appointed to TCD's department of geology, where she was employed by Prof R.G.S. Hudson as a photographic technician. Later she assumed responsibility for the Geological Museum and its extensive collection, and immediately redesigned and updated the displays. She curated and catalogued some 20,000 specimens, and re-organised in particular the mineral collection of which she was especially fond. She was ideally suited to museum work being neat, meticulous and interested in visitors. She was never happier than when showing children around the museum. Years later visitors continued to ask for her, and for many who graduated to employment as professional geologists Veronica and her

K 00316

Síniú an tSealbhóra ⎱
Signature of Holder ⎰   *Veronica Conroy Burns*

Veronica Conroy Burns's wartime Travel Permit Card (1944) showing her photograph and signature. Image: courtesy, Geological Museum, TCD

museum was their first experience of geology.

Veronica Burns's main geological skill was as a fossil collector, and in this she excelled. On Saturday mornings she would take a bus to the collecting localities and spend all day splitting rocks in her search for good specimens, stopping only briefly to eat a sandwich. In the early 1960s she began to collect Silurian graptolites (fossils of colonial marine animals), from the coastal area between Balbriggan and Skerries in north Co. Dublin and from small quarries and exposures inland. These rocks generally contain few fossils, but through her tenacity and patience she was able to assemble a large collection of about 2,000 specimens. Through the influence of Prof Hudson she also focussed on Feltrim Hill, still in north Co. Dublin, where she collected a large number of Lower Carboniferous fossils from the Waulsortian carbonate mudmound and its intercalated shales. These were used by Hudson, Michael Clarke and George Sevastopulo in their 1966 paper published in the *Scientific Proceedings of the Royal Dublin Society*.[29]

Burns kept an album of photographs that she had taken of the quarry at the time, and it contains two fascinating images: one is of the windmill that once stood on top of Feltrim Hill, perched precariously on an isolated tower of limestone around which quarrying had taken place, and the second is of Veronica herself brandishing her hammer at a mechanical digger, and captioned 'The Rivals'. The album and the hammer are now in the TCD Geological Museum, along with her fossil collection.

Veronica Burns was modest about her achievements and only when Barrie Rickards, a graptolite expert, was appointed as a geology lecturer in TCD in 1967, was the importance of her graptolite collection recognised. With Rickards and Jean Archer in 1973 and with Rickards in 1993, Burns published two papers in which her collections were used to determine precisely the age of the rocks around Balbriggan that are 440–420 million years old. In the latter publication a new graptolite subspecies, *Monograptus flemingii* (Salter) *warreni* Burns and Rickards, 1993, was described and illustrated.

Burns was deservedly elected an honorary member of the Irish Geological Association and an honorary life member of the Dublin

'The Rivals': Veronica Burns at Feltrim Quarry, north Co. Dublin c. 1962. Image: courtesy, Geological Museum, TCD

Naturalists' Field Club. Although increasingly incapacitated in the last years of her life, Veronica remained cheerful and interested in the activities of her family and friends. She had a wide circle of friends and colleagues and her enthusiasm for geology and astronomy never wavered.

Associated places
Veronica Conroy Burns: 39 Pembroke Road, Dublin; Geological Museum, Trinity College, Dublin.

Acknowledgements
The role of women geologists in Ireland was the subject of a paper by UCC geologist Dr Bettie Higgs and myself. I would like to acknowledge the help of Kenneth James, Ulster Museum. I am grateful to Philip Doughty (formerly Keeper of Geology, Ulster Museum) who told me about the BNFC collection of erratics in the Ulster Museum, and to Cherry Lewis who supplied me with the photograph of Doris Reynolds and Arthur Holmes for this essay.

Princess of Polytopia: Alicia Boole Stott was an imaginative self-taught mathematician who could visualise shapes in four-dimensions.

The Fabulous Boole Sisters

Two of the five daughters born to logician and mathematician George Boole and his wife, educational psychologist Mary Everest, inherited their parents' interest in science and made their mark in the world – Alicia Boole Stott (1860-1940), an imaginative self-taught mathematician, and Lucy Boole (1862-1905), the first woman professor of chemistry in Britain. A third daughter, Ethel Lilian Voynich (1864-1960) became a revolutionary and a best-selling novelist.

by Prof. Des MacHale and Anne Mac Lellan

The Boole sisters were born in the provincial Irish city of Cork, yet three of them went on to make their mark in a world that did not expect or encourage women to move outside the domestic sphere. The five sisters came into the world at evenly spaced intervals, starting with Mary Ellen, born in 1856, followed at two-yearly intervals by Margaret, Alicia, Lucy, and finally Ethel Lilian in 1864. Alicia was a self-taught mathematician and one of the first people to explore 4-dimensional geometrical figures, for which she was eventually awarded an honorary doctorate. Lucy became the first woman professor of chemistry at the Royal Free Hospital, London. And the youngest, Ethel, went on to become a novelist, music composer and revolutionary. The unusual abilities displayed by these three women are partially explained by their parentage: their father, George, also self-educated, made a major contribution to mathematics that, a century later, made digital computing possible; their mother, Mary, was an eccentric educationalist with a strong interest in mathematics. So unusual was their family history and upbringing, that a little background is warranted.

George Boole appears to have been an interested father, devising a string and card game to teach his children geometrical shapes, and which his widow later commercialised as Boole Curve Sewing Cards. (These were a forerunner of the modern art form of filography in which metal wires are wound around pins to create artistic shapes from mathematical envelopes.) Like many Victorian fathers, George Boole had strict views on discipline and upbringing yet was also an advocate of family peace, claiming that nothing was as important to children's welfare as harmony between their parents, and his own marriage appears to have been happy. However, he was often absent-minded and could be distant while working. George Boole later achieved renown for his Boolean algebra, a way of writing logical arguments in algebraic form so that they can be manipulated, but his beginnings were modest. Born in Lincoln, England, in 1815, the son of a shoemaker and a lady's maid, he was educated at a school for the children of tradesmen and, later, a commercial school, but he had to leave at the age of 16 when his father's business collapsed. His father was interested in science and made optical instruments as a hobby, and taught George mathematics.

With poverty and eccentricity as his birthright, George Boole never had the opportunity to attend either a secondary school or a university as a student. However, this very lack of formal education may have nurtured his innovative approach to problem solving. His work on the algebra of logic was a fundamental step towards the development of the modern digital computer, something that was not realised until 1939 by Claude Shannon at MIT: Boolean algebra provides the basis for assessing true/false logical propositions, and these yes/no statements can be readily translated into the on/off settings in a digital computer. By 1849, despite not having a college education, George Boole's achievements had earned him a certain status and following, and he was appointed the first professor of mathematics in the recently established Queen's College (now University College), Cork. Awarded honorary degrees from the Universities of Dublin (Trinity College), and Oxford, and elected a Fellow of the Royal Society in 1857, he remained in Cork until his untimely death from pneumonia in 1864.

At 37, Boole married Mary Everest, the 20-year-old niece of the surveyor-general of India, Sir George Everest, after whom the mountain is named. Her father was a devoted disciple of Samuel Hahnemann, the founder of homeopathy, and when Mary was five, he moved his family to Paris to be near Hahnemann. The family lived by the homoeopath's tenets, so cold baths and pre-breakfast walks were the order of the day. Mary was interested in mathematics and algebra, which she studied long before she met George. Another uncle of Mary's, John Ryall, was the vice-president and professor of Greek at Queen's College, Cork, and he introduced Mary to George Boole when she visited Cork in

Three of the five Boole sisters: Mary, Margaret and Alicia.

1850. The pair corresponded for a number of years, during which time Boole visited the Everest family in England and tutored Mary in mathematics. They married in 1855, when he was 40 and she was 23, and appear to have enjoyed a happy marriage.

George Boole died in 1864 of inflammation of the lungs, the result of a severe soaking while walking the three miles to college from their home in Ballintemple, Cork. According to some sources, his wife may have played an unwitting part by wrapping him in damp sheets, following the homeopathic principle of the commonality of cause and cure. His wife Mary was widowed at only 32 and his children were still young: Mary, the eldest, was eight, and Ethel Lilian, the youngest, was only six months old.

The family was left almost destitute. Through the efforts of friends, Mary Boole was granted a pension of £100, just enough to allow her to settle her affairs and secure a job as librarian in the Queen's College, London. This institution, founded in 1848, was the first English college to offer higher education to women.

Though the students were all women, the professors were all men, and the college was purely educational in nature – the women could not be conferred with degrees. Along with the job, Mary was given the tenancy of Number 68, Harley Street, where she ran a boarding house for students. Her daughters attended the college's junior school, all but Alicia, who remained in Cork with relatives for some seven years before joining her mother and sisters in London.

Mary Everest Boole had eclectic interests, from psychology to psychic science, spiritualism, mathematics, education, Judaism, and 'true logic', and encouraged her boarders to work through personal problems in encounter groups, predating Freud and Jung. However, she often teetered on the brink of mental instability and, according to one source, ill-health that "assumed the form of temporary derangement" forced her to resign from her post at Queen's College in 1874. An alternative version attributes her dismissal to her 'dangerous ideas'.

Next, Mary took a job as secretary to a friend of her father's, an unusual surgeon and author called James Hinton. Known to his followers as 'the Wizard', Hinton regarded himself as the 'Saviour of Women' in the same way as Christ was considered the 'Saviour of Men'. After Hinton's death in 1875, Mary continued to promote his ideas. She also corresponded with Charles Darwin, was a friend of H.G. Wells, and her house became a meeting place for antivivisectionists, vegetarians, educational psychologists and fringe religious groups. Her youngest daughter, Ethel, remembered the family's acute poverty but also the steady stream of scientists, writers and eccentrics wandering through the house, enlivening conversation and stimulating debate.

When Ethel was eight, she contracted a serious skin infection, erysipelas. It was thought that the Booles' poor living conditions were to blame so, for a change of air, she was sent to live with her paternal uncle Charles in Lancashire. Ethel later described her uncle as a religious fanatic and sadist who beat his children, but merely abused and tormented her by falsely accusing her of misbehaviour, locking her in a room and threatening to put chemicals in her mouth. Ethel remained there for two years and, soon after returning to London, had a nervous breakdown, but was later to draw on these childhood experiences in her fictional novel *Jack Raymond* (1901).

So, the five daughters grew up in an atmosphere charged with weird and wonderful ideas, without their famous father but with a mother who had revolutionary ideas about education, many of which she published in a series of books between 1884 and 1912, including *The Preparation of the Child for Science* (1904). Her collected works, published posthumously in 1932, are a strange collection of writings and teachings that veered from the prosaic – "No child should be given a multiplication table until it has first constructed one" – to the bizarre: "My father believed (and so do I) that every woman becomes at fifty potentially a medium, more or less. The temporary illness from which so many women suffer at this age is the effort of the mediumship to assert itself." Believing that children should manipulate things in order to visualise and understand geometrical objects, she wrote: "… geometric education may begin as soon as the child's hands can grasp objects. Let him have, among his toys, the five regular solids and a cut cone."

None of the five Boole sisters went to university. The fate of the eldest, Mary, is little remarked, but her choice of husband undoubtedly influenced her younger sister, the mathematically-inclined Alicia. Mary married James Hinton's eldest son, Charles Howard Hinton, whose achievements and feats included studying mathematics and physics, teaching in Japan, being arrested for bigamy and inventing an automatic baseball pitcher. Charles wrote a number of books about the fourth dimension, and developed a geometrical method of building wooden models of the three-dimensional cross-sections of four-dimensional solids, involving hundreds of coloured cubes to each of which he assigned a Latin name. This type of mathematical modelling was, of course, not new to the young Boole girls.

Alicia was the only daughter who inherited her father's mathematical talent. Her introduction to mathematics consisted however, in being taught by her mother and reading the first two books of Euclid, yet she developed a creative mathematical imagination. When her brother-in-law introduced her, at age 18, to his little wooden geometric models, she was fascinated and began to experiment with them. Her interest was purely mathematical, as opposed to Charles Hinton's largely mystical interest. She developed an unusual ability to visualise in the fourth dimension, was particularly interested in the convex regular solids in four dimensions, and coined the term 'polytopes' to describe them.

In three dimensions there are five regular polygons or polyhedra, known since ancient Greek times, and called the Platonic solids: the tetrahedron (or pyramid), with four equal triangular faces; the cube (hexahedron), with six square faces; the

Cardboard models, made by Alicia Boole Stott, and representing the three-dimensional cross-sections of her four-dimensional polytopes.

octahedron (eight triangular faces); dodecahedron (12 pentagonal faces); and icosahedron (20 triangular faces). By manipulating models, Alicia Boole discovered that in four dimensions there are six regular 'hypersolids', or as she called them, polytopes, Despite never learning any analytical geometry, she made three-dimensional central cross-sections of all six using Euclidean constructions and synthetic methods. Working alone and as an amateur, she was unaware that the six polytopes had been discovered by Ludwig Schlaefli in 1840, rediscovered by Washington Irving Stingham and other mathematicians, and then by herself. She had constructed her models purely from curiosity, and for a long time nothing came of them. Despite her talent and creativity, circumstances and attitudes towards the education of women meant that she was not allowed to flourish.

Alicia worked as a secretary, married Walter Stott, an actuary, in 1890, and they had two children. Then, some years later, her attention was drawn to a paper by a Dutch mathematics professor in the *Proceedings of the Amsterdam Academy*. Pieter Hendrik Schoute had approached Alicia Boole's problems by purely analytical means, and his results were identical with hers. When she learned of this, Alicia constructed a set of her cardboard models, photographed them and sent the prints to Schoute at Groningen University. So impressed was Schoute that he came to England to visit, and so began a collaboration that continued until his death in 1913. With Schoute's encouragement, Alicia Boole Stott published her main work in two parts, in 1900 and 1910. The first publication relates to her drawing and models, with reference to the three-dimensional central cross-sections of the regular polytopes.

Alice temporarily left her mathematical work when Schoute died, although the following year, 1914, Groningen University conferred her with an honorary doctorate, quite an achievement for this self-taught mathematician. In 1930, after a gap of 16 years, she resumed her work when her nephew, Geoffrey Ingram Taylor, introduced her to a noted geometer, Harold Scott MacDonald (HSM) Coxeter. He was 23 and she was 70, yet they began to collaborate and soon became friends. Coxeter later said, of the woman he called 'Aunt Alicia': "the strength and simplicity of her character combined with the diversity of her interests to make an inspiring friend." Together, they investigated something called the Gosset four-dimensional polytope. Alicia again made models of its sections, and was the first to point out that its vertices lie on the edges of another polytope, dividing them in golden section. She suggested the idea of partial truncation and invented the processes of expansion and contraction, which led her to discover a great variety of uniform polytopes. She and Coxeter delivered a joint paper in Cambridge University, and Alicia donated a set of models for permanent exhibition in the department of mathematics, where they can still be seen. Although they did not publish jointly, in his later work Coxeter often made reference to Alicia and her work.

Alicia Boole Stott died in Middlesex in 1940. The mathematician R.R. Ball, in his *Mathematical Recreations and Essays*, describes her techniques as "extraordinarily fruitful", and one can only speculate about what she might have achieved had her father lived longer and been able to guide her. In the spring of 2001, an old paper roll containing beautifully coloured drawings of polyhedra was found in a basement at Groningen University. The roll was unsigned but the drawings were quickly recognised as Alicia's work. The discovery stimulated research by Irene Polo-Blanco, who devoted a chapter to Alicia's work in her book on the *Theory and History of Mathematical Models* (2007).

Alicia's son Leonard went on to become a pioneer in the treatment of tuberculosis, invented a successful artificial pneumothorax apparatus, a portable X-ray

Russian revolutionary from Cork

ETHEL LILIAN, fifth and youngest Boole daughter, became interested in revolutionary causes when, aged 15, she read about Giuseppe Mazzini, an Italian writer and revolutionary. From then on she dressed in black and preferred to be called Lily. Three years later, she inherited a small legacy that allowed her to pursue her love of music and study at Berlin's Hochschule der Musik. There, she became interested in revolutionary Russia and Eastern Europe. Back in London, she studied Russian with Sergei 'Stepniak' Kravchinski, who had fled to England after murdering the chief of the Tsarist police.

In 1887, Ethel travelled to Russia, stopping en route in Warsaw. In the great square she stared in horror at the city's citadel, which had become a notorious prison. One of the prisoners staring back at the young blonde woman would later become her husband – Wilfred Michail Voynich, a Polish nationalist, was about to be sent to Siberia for helping two political prisoners escape.

After two years in Russia, Ethel returned to London a committed revolutionary, and began meeting other revolutionaries and celebrities such as Eleanor Marx (daughter of Karl), George Bernard Shaw and Oscar Wilde. In 1890, she met Voynich, who had escaped from Siberia and remembered seeing her in Warsaw square. By 1895 they were living together and Ethel styled herself 'E.L.V', though they did not marry until 1902; they later drifted apart, although both moved to New York later in life.

Ethel began to write, and to translate Russian stories. Then, legend has it that she met another Russian exile and spy, Sigmund Rosenblum, one of whose aliases was Sidney Reilly, on whom the James Bond character is supposedly based. Her best-selling 1897 novel, *The Gadfly*, is also allegedly based on Reilly. According to some sources, Ethel and Sidney had a passionate affair, until he abandoned her in Florence; other sources scotch accounts of any affair, on the grounds that Ethel had no sexual interest in men.

The *Gadfly* was widely read by socialists in the West, but in Russia it became the bible of the revolution, selling more than 5 million copies in 22 of the languages of the former USSR. It also sold more than a million copies in China and Eastern Europe, was made into two full-length films, including one with a score by Shostakovich which won an award at the 1955 Cannes film festival, and at least three operatic versions. E.L.V. belatedly received royalties when a Soviet delegation discovered her in New York in 1955 *The Gadfly* is still in print, and arguably sold more copies worldwide than any other book by an Irish-born author.

Today, the Voynich name is also associated with the mysterious 'Voynich manuscript', which Ethel's husband, by then a rare book dealer, acquired in 1912. Now in the

Ethel Lilian Boole or 'E.L.V.'

rare books library at Yale University, and supposedly written in an unknown code, it has been variously attributed to several historical scientists, hoaxers and even aliens.

Lucy Boole, first woman professor of chemistry at the Royal Free Hospital, London

machine and a navigation system based on spherical trigonometry. Alicia's sister Margaret married Edward Ingram Taylor, a well-known artist, and their son Geoffrey (who introduced Alicia to Coxeter), also went on to make his mark. An influential mathematical physicist, he published more than 200 scientific papers covering a range of topics from shock waves to the location of icebergs and the deformation of crystalline materials. In 1933, he was awarded the Royal Society's gold medal, almost a hundred years after his grandfather had received the first such medal for mathematics, and he was knighted in 1944. His interest in science had been stimulated by his aunt, the chemist Lucy Boole, who gave him a small X-ray bulb and he became fascinated by experiments involving X-rays of low intensity.

Lucy, George and Mary Boole's fourth daughter, did not marry and lived with her mother in London. The only one of the five sisters to have a professional career, she studied chemistry and became a lecturer at the London School of Medicine for Women. She collaborated and published jointly with a noted industrial and pharmaceutical chemist, Sir Wyndham Dunstan (1861-1949), director of the UK's Imperial Institute (1903-24). Lucy Boole was a fellow of the Institute of Chemistry and, it is believed, the first woman professor of chemistry at the Royal Free Hospital, London. Her mother pithily summarised her career: "Lucy Everest Boole: never at any college. Learned chemistry in order to qualify as dispenser or shop assistant in pharmacy. Became Fellow of the Institute of Chemistry, Lecturer in Chemistry and Head of Chemical Laboratories at the London School Of Medicine for Women." The tone of this suggests that mother and daughter did not always get on well together. Lucy died in 1905, still in her early 40s and, sadly, little more is known about her life and work.

Thus, George Boole and Mary Everest, two extraordinary people, transmitted their genius not just through their work but also through their descendents. Their children included a mathematician, the so-called Princess of Polytopes, Alicia; a chemist, Lucy, and a novelist and revolutionary, 'E.L.V' (see Panel). Their remaining children, Mary and Margaret, do not appear to have developed careers but their families carried on the Boole Everest tradition: Margaret's son G.I. Taylor becoming a noted mathematical physicist; Mary's granddaughter, Joan Hinton, was a nuclear physicist who worked on the Manhattan Project and witnessed the first atomic explosion in the New Mexico desert. In 1947, shocked by the devastation wrecked by the bombs dropped on Japan, she left the US for communist China. Mary's grandson George Boole Hinton, was an entomologist who published more than 300 papers on taxonomy.

Not many families can claim to have enriched the world of mathematics and science to such an extent. George Boole, his wife and daughters could not boast a single degree among them. George overcame the obstacles poverty put in his way, but his wife and daughters had an additional obstacle to overcome: the gendered expectations that stood in the way of all Victorian women.

*The class entering Girton College Cambridge in 1886,
with Alice Everett (seated, second row, fifth from the left),
and Annie Russell (standing, extreme right). Girton was
the first British women's college of university rank.*
Image: courtesy, Mistress & Fellows, Girton College, Cambridge

Torch-bearing Women Astronomers

Two young women from Northern Ireland were among the first professional women astronomers employed in Ireland or Britain. Annie Dill Russell (1868-1947), later Mrs Maunder, went on to become a renowned observer and photographer of solar eclipses, and an expert in sunspots. Alice Everett (1865-1949) went on to an international career in physics, even inventing equipment for early television technology.

by Dr Máire Brück

The first professional women astronomers in Ireland or Britain were the 'lady computers' employed at the Royal Observatory, Greenwich in the 1890s. Only two of these women persevered to make tangible contributions to science and, coincidentally, both were pioneering Irish women educated in Belfast schools and at Girton College, Cambridge University: Alice Everett and Annie Dill Russell (later Mrs Maunder).[1] They were ahead of their time, and 40 years would elapse before a university-educated woman scientist was appointed to an official position at the Greenwich observatory. Yet these two pioneering women paved the way for other women astronomers and scientists and, despite the professional restrictions of the time, managed to establish international reputations in their chosen field.

Annie Scott Dill Russell (1868-1947) was born in Strabane, Co Tyrone, the daughter of Rev. William Andrew Russell (1824-99), a minister of the Irish Presbyterian Church, and his wife (née Dill) herself the daughter of a minister in the same Church. The family had a devoutly Christian and serious-minded upbringing, and all six children were high-level academic achievers.[2] Annie's only sister Hester (later Smith), qualified with high distinction as a medical doctor under the famous Elizabeth Garret Anderson in the London Hospital for Women. Annie received her secondary education at the Ladies' Collegiate School (later Victoria College), Belfast, won a prize in the Irish Intermediate examination in 1886, and sat the open entrance examination to Girton College Cambridge, gaining a scholarship of £35 annually for three years.

Girton College, the first women's college in Britain of university rank, had been established at Cambridge in 1873. From 1882, women were permitted to sit the Cambridge 'Tripos' (degree) examinations, though they were not granted degrees, a right not conceded until as late as 1948. In 1886, Alice Everett and Annie Russell, aged 21 and 18 respectively, entered Girton College together in an intake of 29 students. Both women attained honours in the mathematical tripos in 1889, and Annie was Girton's top mathematician of her year.

At this time, the Astronomer Royal Sir William Christie was taking a bold step: introducing women to the staff of the Royal Observatory at Greenwich. The observatory's scientific staff consisted then of a number of assistants in charge of the various departments, and a team of 'computers' who did the laborious numerical calculations. There were also several 'supernumerary' computers who were hired as needed, whose posts were temporary and usually taken by school-leaving boys of 13 or 14. It was at this poorly paid bottom rank that the 'lady computers' were recruited.[3] Yet several enthusiastic women grasped the opportunity to take part in scientific duties of any kind and turned these lowly appointments to advantage.

Alice Everett was the first to be appointed in January 1890. Meanwhile, Annie Russell wrote repeatedly to the Astronomer Royal asking to join and was at last offered a post at the lowest salary − £4 a month − much less than she was then earning as a schoolteacher. Nevertheless, she decided to accept, and began work on 1 September 1891. Each woman was assigned to one of the observatory's departments and, in addition, was expected to take their turn in one of the observatory's principal official duties: recording star crossings with the Transit

Annie Maunder and other astronomers in Talni, India, to observe the total solar eclipse of 1898. Annie's husband Walter is on her right. Image: courtesy, Institute of Astronomy, Cambridge

telescope, for astronomical time-keeping. This was night work, and meant traversing Greenwich Park on foot in the dark, a hazardous experience for young women.

Annie was assigned to work in the solar department under its chief (Edward) Walter Maunder. Prompted by the discovery some years before of the 11-year sunspot cycle, this special department had been set up in 1873 for regular photography of the Sun, with Maunder in charge, a post he held all his working life. The project was particularly interested in sunspots: the position of each spot and its apparent area were measured; subsequent calculations converted these observations to standard coordinates, and areas to fractions of the Sun's surface. (Annie and Walter Maunder used this data later to reveal a significant sunspot pattern.) Maunder, though not university educated, was an excellent observer with a world-wide reputation. The routine that Annie followed as his amanuensis entailed photographing the Sun every day through a telescope, weather permitting; then developing the photographs and examining the 8-inch images with a measuring micrometer. Photographs were also taken with similar instruments at observatories in India and Mauritius, and brought to Greenwich, so that the Sun was kept effectively under constant observation. Sunspots come and go in an 11-year cycle, and Annie was fortunate in being appointed at the approach to the sunspot maximum of 1894: she witnessed a famous giant spot of July 1892, and the resulting magnetic storm – a disturbance of the Earth's magnetic field, caused by material emanating from the Sun in a manner not fully understood at the time – was recorded on the observatory's magnetic instruments.

Not content with their prescribed duties, Annie and Alice took every opportunity to learn all they could about the work in the observatory's other departments and made and published observations of eclipses of stars by the Moon, and other phenomena. In 1892, their senior colleagues proposed the two women for admission to the Royal Astronomical Society, a prestigious organisation and the professional body for astronomers of all interests. Unfortunately, their nominations failed to gain the requisite two-thirds support of the all-male Fellows who claimed that women were ineligible. However, Annie and Alice were made welcome in the British Astronomical Association (BAA), a society founded in 1890 by a group of fair-minded individuals, led by Walter Maunder, to cater for lovers of astronomy without discrimination. Annie Russell was to be closely involved with the BAA for the rest of her life, and in 1894 was made editor of the association's journal, a duty she discharged with notable success for 35 years.

For the 1898 eclipse in India Annie used a camera of her own design

On 28 December 1895, Annie Russell married her boss, Walter Maunder, and resigned from her post, presumably because of the bar on married women working in public service at the time. Annie was aged 27, Maunder a widower approaching 45 years of age with a family of five children, ranging in age from seven to 21; Walter and Annie had no children of their own. Although rearing the youngest stepchildren must have taken a great deal of Annie's time and energy, nevertheless she continued to edit the BAA journal and found time for eclipse expeditions. She was soon preparing to accompany her husband on an expedition to Norway to observe the total solar eclipse of 9 August 1896. The weather was unfortunately cloudy at their station and so they saw nothing, but the expedition was a valuable experience for novices such as Annie.

The next total eclipse occurred on 22 January 1898, visible this time in India,

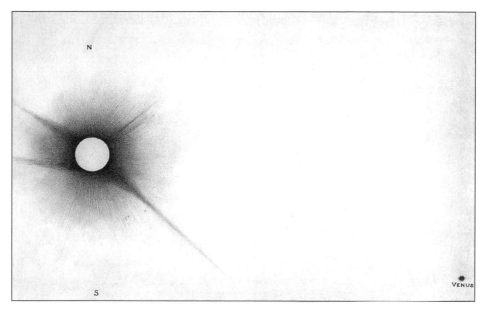

The long coronal ray: Annie Maunder's photograph of the solar corona with the long streamers was taken with her short focus camera at Talni on 22 January 1898. This drawing, by Mr Wesley, secretary of the Royal Astronomical Society, was made from a negative of the photograph. Venus (bottom right), became visible during the eclipse. Image: courtesy, High Altitude Observatory, Boulder, Colorado

and the Maunders were favoured with excellent weather.[4] Each had their own apparatus, and Annie used a short-focus camera of her own design paid for by a grant of £40 from her old college, Girton. It had a lens of just 1.5 inches with a wide field of view that could reach the outermost regions of the corona. Her camera design turned out to be perfect for the task, and reveals a considerable technical expertise and knowledge of optics and mathematics. Working with just a few minutes of eclipse totality, and exposures ranging from 1-20 seconds, she managed to take several excellent photographs. One in particular showed a bright streamer reaching 10 million km into space (14 times the solar radius), and the longest extension of the corona then recorded by any observer. The photograph was widely published in accounts of the eclipse by Walter, but usually under his name. When the results of the various British expeditions were displayed at a Royal Society exhibition in London, the noted Irish-born astronomy writer Agnes Clerke gave her verdict: "As regards the corona, Mrs Maunder with her tiny lens has beaten all the big instruments." The Maunders speculated

A quadrant of the corona photographed in Mauritius during the solar eclipse on 18 May 1901. From the Maunders' book, The Heavens and their Story.

on the significance of this long ray, and suggested that material was being spewed out by the Sun in a stream – an idea ahead of its time and mostly ignored, but subsequently proved correct.

The Maunders took part in two further eclipse expeditions, both favoured with clear skies: to Algiers in May 1900, and to Mauritius the following year. At the latter, Walter was an official observer for the government team while, as before, Annie worked independently. She had an additional project: to photograph the Milky Way by night with her short focus camera, but the moist warm atmosphere caused dew to form continuously on her lens and made photography impossible. Her eclipse instrument now was a more conventional camera with which she produced a set of excellent corona photographs, showing a most delicate pattern of plumes and prominences.[5] Now regarded as an expert on eclipse photography, she was invited to join and take charge of corona photography on the Canadian government's eclipse expedition to Labrador in August 1905, the only time her expedition expenses were paid, but unfortunately the weather was cloudy.

The Maunder name is mostly associated in astronomy today with the 'butterfly diagram', an elegant graphical analysis of the 11-year sunspot cycle which revealed how the latitude of sunspots proceeds regularly with each cycle. The diagram resembled three butterflies, one for each of the cycles the Maunders analysed. They graphed the latitude of each spot against the date of observation, working at home, as Annie recalled years later: "We made this diagram in a week of evenings, one dictating and the other ruling these little lines. We had to do it in a hurry because we wanted to get it before the [Royal Astronomical] Society at the same meeting as the other sunspot observers, whose views we knew to be heretical. As it turned out . . . the diagram wiped the other papers clean off the slate."[6]

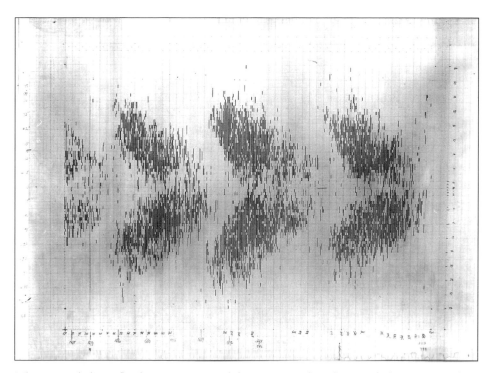

The original 'butterfly diagram': prepared by Annie and Walter Maunder in 'a week of evenings' in 1904, it reveals how sunspot location varies periodically with each sunspot cycle. Image: courtesy, High Altitude Observatory, Boulder, Colorado

The striking diagram was more illuminating than a thousand words. The distinctive progress of the cycle was plain to see – the spots' downward drift in latitude as the cycle progresses, and the beginning of a fresh cycle before the old one vanishes. The same butterfly-shaped pattern repeats itself each cycle: today, a century later, a dozen 'butterflies' have been born and passed on. It is one of the best known and most delightful diagrams in astronomy. Walter published the diagram in a paper in 1904, and it was generally attributed to him alone.[7] It has taken 100 years for Annie's part to become known through the efforts of Dr Tom Bogdan of the High Altitude Observatory, Boulder, who had the original drawing restored and its history revealed in 2000.

The Maunders were also interested in a 70-year calm period in the 17th century when sunspots were scarce, first identified by a German astronomer Gustav Spörer but known today as the 'Maunder minimum'. The Maunders confirmed that when sunspots are scarce, there are also few if any magnetic disturbances and auroral displays ('northern lights'). The 'Maunder minimum' has taken on a new importance in recent debates about climate change and the Sun's influence on our weather.

Another important discovery the Maunders made was that magnetic storms on Earth recur in 27-day cycles. As seen from the Earth, on average the Sun rotates on its axis once in about 27 days, bringing any disturbed area on the Sun round to face the Earth with that frequency, even though nothing special may be visible. The Maunders correctly concluded that the culprit was not on the Sun's obvious face but in the corona, and only in recent decades has their contribution been reassessed and appreciated.[8] Annie independently made use of the Greenwich records to compile other sunspot statistics which were published in the official Royal Observatory reports.[9] Like her husband, she also came out against the then popular acceptance of artificial 'canals' on Mars.[10]

In 1910 the Maunders published a popular book, *The Heavens and their Story*, Annie's name appearing as the first author on the title page.[11] In a preface, Walter admits that the book "which stands in the joint names of my wife and myself, is almost wholly the work of my wife, as circumstances prevented me taking any further part in it soon after it was commenced." That it was not published under Annie's sole name as would have been proper, demonstrates women's still unequal position in society, and perhaps the fact that Walter was better known. This delightful book displays Mrs Maunder's style and interests, and is illustrated with photographs and drawings, including Annie's own photographs of the Indian and Mauritius eclipses. Annie also wrote many popular articles and gave occasional lectures, though she did not enjoy speaking in public.

Although Annie was more qualified than her husband, arguably her scientific career was somewhat hampered by him. He had held the same rank at Greenwich for 30 years while smart younger men with university degrees overtook him. Instead, he built his empire among the amateur astronomers in the British Astronomical Association. As a result, Annie's eclipse observations were published under Walter's name in popular journals rather than broadcast throughout the professional community and, not being herself a Fellow of the Royal Astronomical Society, she could not submit her work there on her own account. Some professional scientists ignored the amateurs altogether.[12] Yet, as Marilyn Ogilvie, a modern historian of astronomy and an admirer of Annie, points out, a career as an "obligatory amateur" was the only one open to her, and she made the most of

"I have eclipse-hunted in queer places, but I have never climbed mountains nor ski-ed on the eternal snow." Signature: courtesy, University of Colorado at Boulder, library archives.

it.[13] She had, of course, the advantage over other amateurs that the Greenwich solar records were available to her.

Walter Maunder retired in 1913 after 40 years of service. A year later, World War I broke out and the Royal Observatory, in common with many British institutions, found itself short of staff as its male workers left on active service. In 1916, Maunder (then aged 66) was recalled to his old post in charge of the Greenwich sunspot records. His wife joined him as an unpaid volunteer, and the couple kept up their solar work until 1920, well after the end of the war. Meantime, in 1915, the ban on women in the Royal Astronomical Society was finally lifted, and Annie was made a Fellow, more than 20 years after her name had first been put forward, a fact that she did not allow her male colleagues to forget.

Walter Maunder died in 1928 after a long illness. Annie, though bereft of her husband and professional partner of 33 years, continued to devote herself to the BAA's work and to historical research. Working from translations, she studied astronomical references in Iranian and Indian sacred texts;[14] looked into cometary records in the writings of 17th-century traveller, Peter Mundy, and wrote an astronomical appendix to a new printing of his works; and researched the origins of the constellation names and their possible dates.[15] She was looked on in her lifetime as an expert in the field.

The 50th anniversary of the BAA's founding saw Annie still active. She and a colleague and friend, Mrs Mary Evershed, despite the difficult conditions of

World War II, responded to a request to write the association's history. Annie, now aged 74, delivered a paper on 30 September 1942 in which she recalled the friendly spirit that inspired its foundation, and which she herself had done so much to sustain. "Men and women astronomers came in on equal terms; so also with the rich and the poor; those who worked with their hands and those with their heads; and all pooled their varying knowledge for the public good."[16]

Annie remained in touch with solar astronomers, including a young man who later rose to eminence, Walter Orr Roberts, at the High Altitude Observatory in Colorado, which specialised in observations of the Sun. At the height of the war, when London was under threat of invasion, Annie sent him the original 'butterfly diagram' and an enlarged drawing of her 'longest coronal ray' for safe keeping. These historic items are preserved and displayed in the Colorado observatory today. Annie Maunder survived her husband by almost 20 years, dying on 15 September 1947 in her 80th year. The Maunders are individually commemorated by craters on the Moon – a unique case for a couple. Annie herself would probably choose to be remembered by her most cherished pieces of work: the butterfly diagram and the longest coronal ray.

Alice Everett (1865-1949), who grew up in Belfast, was the first 'lady computer' employed at the Royal Observatory Greenwich, and arguably the first professional woman astronomer in Ireland or Britain. She excelled at mathematics and physics, and went on to have a varied career in physics and later television technology, although we know somewhat less about her life and work than we do about her colleague and contemporary, Annie Mauder. Everett's choice of subject and career is perhaps not surprising, as her father, Joseph David Everett FRS (1831-1904), was Professor of Natural Philosophy (science) at Queen's College Belfast (now Queen's University Belfast). Alice was educated at Belfast Methodist College, a co-educational day school, and then at Queen's College Belfast which from 1882 allowed women to take lectures there in preparation for the Royal University of Ireland examinations, though the Belfast College did not fully recognise the women students. Following a brilliant record at Queen's,[17] Alice proceeded to Girton College, where she was a contemporary of Annie Russell and, like her, achieved honours in the mathematical Tripos (degree) examination.

While there she also sat and passed with honours the Royal University of Ireland's Master of Arts degree in mathematics and mathematical physics.

When Alice took up her position at Greenwich, she was assigned to a new project, the Astrographic Catalogue and Chart or *Carte du Ciel*, an ambitious international plan to photograph and survey the entire celestial sky and to catalogue all stars above a certain brightness on those photographs. These were early days in astronomical photography, and the novel enterprise attracted great excitement. Eighteen of the world's best resourced observatories agreed to share the sky among them, each responsible from start to finish for its allotted zone. Many of these observatories employed teams of women as cheap labour in the last tedious steps of this process; at Greenwich, however, Alice was involved in every stage: she took the actual photographs, sometimes observing for up to seven hours a night at a stretch, and her contribution is recorded in the published catalogue. As a sideline and for her own interest she learned to handle other telescopes at the observatory, and made observations of the 'nova' or new star of 1892,[18] and published a catalogue of observations of double stars.[19]

Alice Everett was probably one of the first people to see a television image

After five years at Greenwich, Alice moved in 1895 to the Astrophysical Observatory in Potsdam, Europe's leading astrophysical research institution, becoming the first woman employed at a German observatory. Next, she crossed the Atlantic and spent a year at the observatory of Vassar College, Poughkeepsie, USA, America's first all-women university.[20] The director of Lick Observatory in California was most anxious to recruit her as a spectroscopist, but could not find the funds. Posts in astronomy were few, even in the United States and in 1900, at the age of 35, Alice returned to Britain. This marked the end of her career in astronomy, and from now on her principal scientific interest was optics, although she remained an active amateur member of the British Astronomical Association.

Alice Everett next spent a period at the Davy-Faraday Laboratory in London's prestigious Royal Institution, a laboratory set up for scientists who lacked facilities elsewhere to carry out experiments. She was the only woman to have been accommodated there.[21] The outcome was a paper on zonal aberrations in lenses, which her father communicated to the Physical Society of London, and which had the distinction of being the first by a woman to appear in the *Proceedings of the Physical Society*. She also collaborated with her father on translating, from German, a weighty technical monograph on Jena glass (a high-quality glass ideal for optical, scientific and industrial uses).[22] Alice then took an advanced course in practical optics at the Technical College, South Kensington, and spent a year with the optical firm of Hilgers in London. Her career opportunity came during World War I when women were recruited into formerly male occupations to replace men who were absent on active service. Alice joined the staff of the National Physical Laboratory in 1917 as a research scientist in its optical laboratory, her special field being theoretical calculations of aberrations in lens and mirror systems. Her success in these original researches may be judged from her scientific publications listed in the *Annual Reports of the National Physical Laboratory*.[23] In 1925, she left the National Physical Laboratory on reaching the statutory retiring age of 60, but this indomitable woman now embarked on a new field of interest.

During the next two years (1926-28), Alice studied practical wireless at Regent Street Polytechnic, London, and passed the College's examinations in 'wireless, HF and AC measurements', undertook research in the electrical engineering department of the City and Guilds College (now Imperial College), and became an associate of the Institute of Radio Engineers. Her most fascinating activity was her involvement with new technology of television. On 26 January 1926, the Scottish engineer and inventor John Logie Baird gave the first demonstration in Britain, and reputedly the first in the world, of a television image. The demonstration took place in a garret in Soho, London, to an invited audience of 40 guests, among them two women scientists. Alice Everett may have been, indeed probably was, one of those present. The following year, the Television

Signature: courtesy, Royal Greenwich Observatory archives, Cambridge University library RGO 7/138

Society for the promotion of television research came into being. Alice was one of its 325 foundation members, or 'Fellows', and she remained an active member for the rest of her life.

The Baird Television Company was associated with the British Broadcasting Corporation (BBC) from 1929 until 1935, during which time the company pioneered and developed television receiving and transmitting apparatus. Among the inventions was a 'mirror drum' for producing the necessary scanning light beam. Alice Everett suggested certain improvements to Baird's version of this device,[24] and in 1933 she and the company jointly applied to patent the invention. Unfortunately, the BBC did not give Baird the final contract, and the new drum was never constructed. Alice Everett continued to give enthusiastic service to the Television Society. In 1938 she was awarded a civil list (i.e. government) pension of £100 a year in recognition of her own and her father's contributions to physical science. She died in London on 29 July 1949, aged 84, leaving her library of scientific books to the Television Society.

Acknowledgements

I would like to record the help of the late Sheelagh Grew (1931-2006) of Armagh Observatory who was so generous with her knowledge of local Ulster history.

FORM OF RESEARCH LICENCE.

THERAPEUTIC SUBSTANCES ACT, 1932.

Licence No. 44 (R).

The Minister for Local Government and Public Health in exercise of the powers conferred on him by the above mentioned Act, hereby licenses —

Dorothy Price, M.B., B.Ch.,

of

St. Ultan's Infant Hospital, Charlemont Street, Dublin,

being a person engaged in scientific research, to import for the purpose of scientific research at —

St. Ultan's Infant Hospital, Dublin,

or in such other place or places as the said Minister may from time to time authorise, the under-mentioned therapeutic substance from:

Dr. Wassen's Laboratory, Goteborg, Sweden,

namely: B.C.G. Preventative Tuberculin Vaccine in single doses in sealed ampoules.

This licence is granted subject to the conditions pertaining to the importation of therapeutic substances for the purpose of scientific research set out in any Regulations made under the said Act and for the time being in force and may be suspended or revoked by the said Minister if the licensee is convicted of an offence under the said Act.

This licence will, unless previously suspended or revoked by the said Minister, continue in force for a period of two years from the date hereof.

Given under the Official Seal of the Minister for Local Government and Public Health this 5th. day of December, in the year One Thousand Nine Hundred and Thirty-Six.

Seán T. O'Ceallaigh

Minister for Local Government and Public Health.

Dr Dorothy Stopford Price introduced the BCG vaccine to Ireland: this 1936 licence to import allowed her to conduct the first Irish trial of the vaccine's efficacy, at St Ultan's clinic in 1937. Image: courtesy, Trinity College Dublin, MS 7534/154/2

Revolutionary
Doctors

Three revolutionary women doctors made important contributions
to public health in Ireland: Dr Kathleen Lynn (1874-1955) co-
founded the first Irish hospital dedicated to infants; Dorothy
Stopford Price (1890-1954) introduced the BCG vaccine into
Ireland; Brigid Lyons Thornton (1896-1987) specialised in public
health medicine. All three were deeply influenced by the 1916
Rising in Dublin, and their lives were linked by tuberculosis.

by Anne Mac Lellan

April 23rd, Easter Sunday, 1916: *A Sunny Day*

An armed uprising plunges the centre of Dublin city into bloody chaos. Two
officers of the Irish Citizen Army, Dr Kathleen Lynn and Countess Markievicz,
share a car carrying first aid supplies into town. The Countess is deployed to St
Stephen's Green while Dr Lynn is posted to City Hall.[1] Lynn describes the scene
in her diary: "It was a beautiful day, the sun was hot and we were not long there
when we noticed Sean Connolly coming towards us, walking upright, although
we had been advised to crouch and take cover as much as possible. We suddenly
saw him fall mortally wounded by a sniper's bullet from [Dublin] Castle. First aid
was useless. He died almost immediately."[2] Following the subsequent death of

Captain John (Jack) O'Reilly, Lynn, chief medical officer and herself a Captain, became the highest ranking officer of the Irish Citizen Army in City Hall.

'In 1911, there were just 33 women doctors in Ireland'

That same Sunday, Brigid Lyons, a young medical student and committed republican, was home in Longford on holiday from her studies in University College Galway. Rumours were rife in Longford and, as tensions mounted, the British army remained out of sight behind the walls of the local barracks.[3] A notice by Eoin MacNeill, chief of staff of the Irish Volunteers, in the previous day's *Irish Independent* stated: "Owing to the very critical position, all orders given to the Irish Volunteers for tomorrow, Easter Sunday, are hereby rescinded, and no parades, marches, or other movements of Irish volunteers will take place." No-one in Longford was quite sure what was so 'critical'. Unknown to Lyons, her uncle Joe MacGuinness was already one of those occupying the Four Courts in Dublin.

Meanwhile, Dorothy Stopford, who hoped to study medicine in Trinity College Dublin (TCD), noted in her diary for Easter Sunday that she bicycled to early service.[4] Stopford was staying in the Phoenix Park with Sir Matthew Nathan, Under-secretary to the British administration in Dublin Castle. Like Lyons, she knew there was trouble afoot but was also unsure as to what was happening so she, too, turned to the newspapers. "Hasty scanning of paper before we saw it. Back just in time for breakfast. Lots of telephoning going on. At 1oc we motored off to lunch; stopped for about half hour at the Castle on the way…Sir M out on business almost all day…"

April 24th, Easter Monday, 1916: *Another lovely sunny morning*
Stopford re-read the weekend newspapers and found a few censored remarks in *The Freeman's Journal* about gun running and thought it might be a clue to what was happening. She, Mrs Nathan (Sir Matthew's sister-in-law) and the children walked to a part of the Phoenix Park known as 'the furry glen' and enjoyed the sun. On their return, a phone call from the Vice Regal Lodge (now Aras an Uachtaráin) informed them that 'the Sinn Féiners were out', that Dublin Castle was surrounded but Sir Matthew was safe.

Meanwhile, an early morning excursion train left Longford for Dublin and the Fairyhouse races in Co Meath. This being a public holiday, there were no newspapers, and everyone in Longford hoped the train's return would bring news of events in Dublin. The platform at Longford railway station that night was crowded, but the train did not arrive until midnight, and with it the news that Sackville Street (Dublin's main street, now O'Connell Street) was burning and the air over it was thick with flying bullets. The Lyons family talked late into the night and Brigid slept badly when she did go to bed.

In Dublin city centre, the General Post Office (GPO), Four Courts, and City Hall were all under attack. Bullets cut the air. Fires broke out. Barricades were erected. Dead horses piled up in Sackville Street. A small part of the city was in revolution. And Dr Kathleen Lynn was at the epicentre. Historian Dr Margaret Ó hÓgartaigh says that Lynn's "quiet yet authoritative manner" as well as her "serene faith" helped to sustain her throughout the day in City Hall, tending to casualties and comforting the wounded.

April 24th, Easter Tuesday, 1916: *Still more brilliant sunshine*

Stopford, bored with being confined to the Phoenix Park, wrote in her diary: "I got up and decided not to try for 9oc lecture but to go down at 10 to the Botany lab...prevented by Mrs N...it was very fussy but I had to give in...it's awfully silly doing nothing...Maude and I went for a walk and posted some letters at the Castleknock Gate. On our way home, to our horror we saw five men drawn across the road, signalling with a white flag." She thought they were about to be ambushed. "...Using glasses we found our five Sinn Féiners were aged road-menders wielding their tools and spades and picks and talking to a young lady holding a bicycle and wearing a white jersey. We are much chaffed for our imaginative vision."

While Stopford was bored, Lyons, her uncle Frank McGuinness and three others left Longford to drive to Dublin. At McKee barracks, to the north of Dublin city, they were told the car could go no further. Lyons noticed a pall of smoke hanging over the city centre. In Bolton Street they met the first barricades, which included sofas, go-carts and Guinness barrels. Lyons and her uncle made it through to the Four Courts where she joined members of the women's organisation, Cumann na mBan, in the basement cooking and making tea. She put her budding surgical skills to use, employing a bayonet to cut up meat.

April 29-30th: *Surrender*

During the week of the Rising, Brigid Lyons was redeployed from the Four Courts to No 5 Church Street where she tended to casualties, made tea and again cut up mutton with a bayonet. When it became clear that defeat was imminent, she made her way to the Four Courts where she was apprehended, still wearing the same good Easter Sunday suit she had worn leaving Longford that Monday. She was subsequently imprisoned in Kilmainham Gaol but obtained early release in May, returned to her studies in Galway, later transferred to University College Dublin (UCD), and qualified as a doctor in 1922.

Lynn, as the highest ranking officer at City Hall, tendered the surrender there. When taken prisoner, her surgical bag contained iodine, lint, bandages, and 50 rounds of ammunition. Asked if she was there in a medical capacity, she is supposed to have replied that she was there as a "Red Cross doctor and a belligerent".[5] She, too, was sent to Kilmainham Goal. In the aftermath of the Rising, 15 men were executed but no women. However, 90 women were imprisoned and six were sent to England: Kathleen Lynn, Constance Markievicz, Helena Molony, Marie Perolz, Kathleen Clarke and Brigid Foley. Lynn returned to Ireland by the end of 1916 and became a member of the Sinn Féin executive in 1917.

Dorothy Stopford's diary for April–May 1916, now in the National Library of Ireland, provides an insight into the 1916 Rising from the Unionist perspective. The aftermath of the Rising radically altered her political views, however. Historian Leon Ó Broin states that she was one of a vast number who changed their allegiance then on account of the execution of the 1916 leaders, the murder, by a British Army officer, of a noted pacifist Francis Sheehy-Skeffington, and the threat of conscription.[6] By the time Stopford qualified as a doctor in 1921 she was a nationalist.

The three women's very different experiences of 1916 were due in part to their age, experience and upbringing. Lyons was the youngest, at 20, a medical student in Galway, a self-described 'fat country girl', and from a Catholic family with strong Republican credentials. Stopford was 26, a middle-class Irish Protestant, the daughter of an accountant, partly educated in St Paul's Girls School, London, and about to embark on the study of medicine at TCD. The dominant ideology among the Protestant minority in Ireland at the time was Unionism, and Dorothy was probably aligned with the British point of view, although she was not particularly interested in politics, according to Ó Broin. Lynn was 42, an Irish Protestant, the daughter of a Church of Ireland clergyman, an advocate of fresh air and cold baths and, at the time of the Rising, a fellow of the Royal College of Surgeons in Ireland. She had been a suffragette, then a socialist and, by 1916, a Republican.

1922–23: *Civil War*

Following the War of Independence, Ireland split into those who supported the Treaty of December 1921 with Britain (which partitioned the country), and those against. Civil war ensued. Returning to her studies in Galway, Brigid Lyons set up a branch of Cumann na mBan. On the pro-Treaty side, and attached to the Longford Brigade under General Sean MacEoin, she was promoted to Commandant and was at times personally responsible to Michael Collins, the legendary Irish revolutionary leader.[7] She later became the first woman commissioned officer in the Irish army, with the rank of First Lieutenant.

Dr Lynn was elected to the Sinn Féin Executive in 1917 – no mean feat, according to her biographer Margaret Ó hÓgartaigh, as there were over 100 candidates and only four women were elected to the 24-person executive. Lynn attempted to keep women's rights to the fore. On May 18th, 1918, she noted in her diary the "whole executive arrested and deported. Myself on the run." When the terms of the Treaty were made clear in December 1921, Lynn raged: "[…] better war than such a peace." Earlier, during July and August that year, Lynn was based in counties Waterford and Tipperary where she showed herself willing to countenance violence in pursuit of political ends. Politically, she lost when the Treaty was signed. In 1923 she was elected for Sinn Féin to the Dáil (Parliament), but along with the other anti-Treaty campaigners she refused to take her seat. Later, she did not join Fianna Fáil nor compromise her views. Instead, she retreated from national politics and concentrated her energies on local government, public health and Teach Ultain or St Ultan's hospital for infants, which she co-founded with Madeleine ffrench-Mullen.[8]

Dorothy Price, despite a close sympathy and personal friendship with members of the British administration in Ireland, emerged as an active nationalist and became medical officer to the IRA's brigade in Cork, probably the most violent of all the counties in its bloody struggle.[9] On Cumann na mBan's instructions, she taught first aid to the Kilbrittain branch, which was closely associated with the activities of the IRA's West Cork brigade and its flying column. Her knowledge of the IRA's activities was extensive — her short history of the IRA in Cork, preserved in the National Library of Ireland, demonstrates an intimate knowledge of their operations.[10]

1921: UK's first woman medical professor
By Laura Kelly

THE FIRST woman appointed as a medical professor in Ireland or Britain was **Dame Anne Louise McIlroy** (1874-1968), from Co Antrim, who was appointed Professor of Obstetrics and Gynaecology at the London School of Medicine for Women in 1921. Like Lynn, Lyons-Thornton and Stopford-Price, her life was influenced by the battlefield.

McIlroy was born in Ballycastle, where her father Dr James McIlroy was a medical doctor, and she and her younger sister Janie followed their father into medicine. They studied at Glasgow University, Anne Louise qualifying with a Bachelor of Medicine and Surgery degree in 1898 and an MD degree two years later, while Janie earned her first degree in 1904. After postgraduate studies in Europe, Anne Louise returned to Scotland specialising in obstetrics and gynaecology.

During World War I women were not permitted on the battlefield, but McIlroy joined the Scottish Women's Hospital for Foreign Service and commanded hospital units in France, Serbia and Salonika, established a nurses' training school in Serbia, and helped to establish the Eastern Army's only orthopaedic centre. The end of the war saw her as a surgeon at a Royal Army Medical Corps hospital in Turkey. She was decorated with several honours for her wartime service, including the French *Croix de Guerre* and an OBE.

In 1921, McIlroy was appointed professor of obstetrics and gynaecology at the University of London, making her the UK's first woman professor of medicine. There was considerable opposition to the appointment, but McIlroy persisted. She was an inspiring teacher and, during her tenure, examination results were consistently above average. She and her assistants also conducted much original research, and she wrote extensively on subjects such as toxaemia in pregnancy and pain relief. McIlroy also worked as a surgeon at the Marie Curie Hospital for Women, and in 1929 was promoted to a Dame of the British Empire for services to midwifery.

She retired from medicine in 1934 but remained busy, studying for a D.Sc. at London University and a legal degree at Glasgow, continuing in practise at Harley

Dame Anne Louise McIlroy, from Co Antrim, 'laid the foundations for a tradition of good teaching in obstetrics and gynaecology'. Image: University of Glasgow Archives, CH4/4/2/2/318.

Street, and as consultant to the Bermondsey Medical Mission and the Thorpe Coombe Maternity Hospital. During World War Two, Dame Louise offered her services again and helped to organise emergency maternity services. A president of the obstetrical section of the Royal Society of Medicine, among other things, it was said that she had 'great personal charm and striking appearance', and that she 'laid the foundations for a tradition of good teaching in obstetrics and gynaecology'. She died in February, 1968, at the age of 93. A new ward for gynaecological patients at the Royal Free Hospital in London was named after her.

Sources: Obituary, *British Medical Journal*, Feb 17, 1968, p.451-454; Obituary, *The Lancet*, Feb 24, 1968, p.371-432; Glasgow University student matriculation albums, 1880-1900.

From war to peace

According to the census, in 1911 there were 33 qualified women doctors and 68 women medical students in Ireland. However, a significant percentage of these went abroad to the religious missions. This may have reflected the limitations they faced at home, the strength of their religious influence, or what historian Myrtle Hill calls the "personal impulse to serve".[11] Women made little inroads into the other professions – the 1911 census records one woman architect and no women lawyers. Women were first admitted to the UK medical register (which included the island of Ireland then) in 1876. It was another 20 years before the first women doctors qualified in Ireland: in 1896, six women students enrolled in the Catholic University Medical School, in Cecilia Street, Dublin, of whom four were Protestant (the school, which opened in 1855, later became UCD's medical school). During the 1890s, 35 women qualified as medical practitioners in Irish medical schools.[12]

Kathleen Lynn began her medical studies in 1894, when she was 20 years old, at the Catholic University Medical School. TCD would have been a more natural choice for a Protestant, but it did not admit women until 1904. Lynn enrolled at the Adelaide Hospital in 1895 and came first in practical anatomy in 1896, the first time a woman gained this distinction; two years later, she was awarded the Barker anatomical prize; and on graduation in 1899, won the Hudson Prize for the Adelaide student with highest marks in the final medical examination. Brigid Lyons enrolled in UCG to study medicine in 1915. One year later, Dorothy Stopford enrolled in TCD. By 1926, there were 208 women doctors in the Irish Free State, and by 1946 that figure had doubled to 430. Stopford, Lyons and Lynn were members of an elite group within an elite section of society, in being able to attend university. However, it may not have seemed all that privileged to those early women doctors. In particular, few Irish hospitals then were willing to employ women doctors, some citing the lack of 'appropriate' accommodation for in-house residents.

Dr Kathleen Lynn was the first woman to be elected as a resident doctor at the Adelaide Hospital, but the staff opposed her appointment and she did not go into residence. However, she subsequently worked in Dublin's Rotunda Maternity Hospital, the Royal Victoria Eye and Ear, and Sir Patrick Dun's (1906-1916). In 1909, after postgraduate study in the USA, Lynn became the third woman awarded the fellowship of the Royal College of Surgeons in Ireland. Stopford initially found it difficult to secure a job, but St Ultan's hospital, co-founded by Lynn, would later provide her with the ideal conditions for her research. Lyons, who was on the winning political side after the Civil War, was able to use her contacts to secure her first temporary position.

Kathleen Lynn and St Ultan's

Kathleen Lynn, like many of her suffragette contemporaries, established a lasting political and domestic relationship with another woman, Madeleine ffrench-Mullen, and together they set up St Ultan's hospital for infants in 1919. They also lived together for almost three decades and biographer Marie Mulholland believes that they loved one another deeply and passionately.[13]

St Ultan's has been aptly described, by another Lynn biographer, Ó hÓgartaigh, as a "women's medical republic". The first Irish clinic specialising in infant care, it was staffed and run entirely by women in its early years. As such, it was unique in Ireland. Men were employed for specialities, but the hospital exercised positive discrimination in favour of women. This was probably a response to the fact that elsewhere women were routinely denied the professional opportunities afforded to their male colleagues. St Ultan's hospital also had a very real purpose: to tackle the high mortality rates among Dublin infants. It began with two cots and a very tight budget, but nine years later there were plans to expand cot numbers to 34. The minutes of the 1928 annual report, note that:

Dr Kathleen Lynn, who co-founded the first Irish hospital dedicated to infant care. A captain in the Irish Citizen Army, she described herself in 1916 as a "Red Cross doctor and a belligerent". Image: courtesy, Royal College of Physicians of Ireland

" . . . the objects of Teach Ultain were to provide treatment in an institution for babies under one year old, suffering from non-infectious diseases including summer diarrhoea, to train nurses for infants, and give opportunities for research into the disorders and the nutrition of infants. "

In the outpatient clinics, Lynn advised mothers about the importance of regular feeding, fresh air, and hygiene – all very difficult to achieve in a city where many families lived in single-room slum accommodation. St Ultan's was one of the first, if not the only hospital in the world to have a Montessori ward and Dr Maria Montessori visited the hospital in 1934. St Ultan's grew and expanded and, in 1949, thanks to the work of Dorothy Price, a BCG block was opened to administer the *Bacille Calmette Guerin*, a French vaccine against tuberculosis (TB).

Kathleen Lynn worked at St Ultan's until the spring of 1955 when she attended her last clinic, despite being 81 and ill. She died that September. St Ultan's continued until the 1980s; the site at Dublin's Charlemont St is currently occupied by a private medical clinic.

Stopford Price and tuberculosis

The existence of a TB epidemic in Ireland was officially recognised in 1841.[14] The epidemic peaked in 1904 when 16% of all deaths were attributed to the infection. Although the incidence began to decline somewhat, TB remained Ireland's most pressing public health problem until the 1950s. Memoirs and biographies of two men – Dr Noel Browne and Dr James Deeny – dominate the historiography of the fight to eradicate TB in the Republic of Ireland in the 1940s and 1950s.[15] A more balanced account is contained in Professor Greta Jones's study of tuberculosis in the 19th and 20th centuries, which includes a brief discussion of the contribution made by Dorothy Price (known as Stopford Price following her marriage in 1925 to a barrister and district justice Liam Price). However, this author believes that Price's contribution to the virtual eradication of TB in the Republic ranks with the achievements of Browne and Deeny, medical doctors who also made their mark in politics and policy. Price remained a medical practitioner and researcher throughout her career and, perhaps as a result, her contribution has been overlooked.

Price engaged with the country's most pressing public health problem, in the

Dr Ada English

ANOTHER woman who made significant contributions to Irish political life and medicine was **Adeline (Ada) English** (1873-1944). During her four decades at Ballinasloe District Lunatic Asylum, Co Galway, where she was medical superintendent, she helped to develop psychiatric services and introduced several then-novel therapies, such as occupational therapy and convulsive treatment, according to psychiatrists Brendan Kelly and Mary Davoren (Mater Hospital, Dublin), who are researching her life. Dr English graduated from the Catholic University School of Medicine, Dublin, in 1903. Deeply involved in Irish politics, she participated in the 1916 Easter Rising, spent six months in Galway jail for possessing nationalist literature (1921), was one of six women elected in 1921 to the second Dáil Éireann as a TD (member of Parliament); and participated in the Civil War (1922).

days before effective antibiotics. Among the interventions that had not yet been tried in Ireland, perhaps the most significant was the BCG vaccine, a live attenuated (weakened) strain of the TB bacterium, *Mycobacterium bovis*, which had been developed by two French researchers, Leon Calmette and Camille Guerin, between 1906 and 1924. Price introduced BCG vaccination to Ireland in 1937, vaccinating infants in St Ultan's Hospital, Dublin.[16] Most evidence indicates that BCG vaccination of children results in a 60-80% decrease in the incidence of the disease.[17] Had the BCG vaccine had been made available on a nationwide basis in the late 1930s, as Stopford Price wished, it would undoubtedly have accelerated the decline of TB, particularly among children. However, it took a decade before vaccination was accepted, but Dorothy Stopford Price's work with the BCG helped its eventual rapid rollout after the government finally adopted it in the late 1940s.

> *'BCG vaccination in Ireland will always be linked with the name of Dr Dorothy Price'*

Dorothy Price on her graduation: in the 1930s and '40s she engaged with the country's most pressing public health problem, tuberculosis, in the days before effective antibiotics. Image: courtesy, Trinity College Dublin, MS 7534/5

In addition to her BCG work, Stopford Price researched and published widely on tuberculosis in children, including an MD thesis (1935) on 'The diagnosis of primary tuberculosis of the lungs in childhood', and numerous articles in peer-reviewed journals such as the *British Medical Journal, British Journal of Tuberculosis, Archives of Disease in Childhood, Tubercle,* and the *Irish Journal of Medical Science.* She wrote a standard textbook on childhood TB,[18] corresponded widely with other international experts such as Walter Pagel and Aarvid Wallgren,[19] and was instrumental in attempting to establish the Irish Anti-Tuberculosis League. Modelled along similar lines to the Swedish league, following suggestions made to Price by Swedish expert Aarvid Wallgren, this provided the impetus for a more effective TB policy in Ireland.

Price's role in establishing the league has been largely ignored. The association was, to all intents and purposes, sabotaged by Rev Dr John Charles McQuaid (then the Catholic Archbishop of Dublin), and other Catholics who opposed it on religious grounds. Yet historian Greta Jones believes that the attempted foundation of the all-Ireland Anti-Tuberculosis League in 1942 was partially responsible for a change of direction in Ireland and the subsequent formulation of a more adventurous TB policy. Much of the credit for this association belongs to Stopford Price, who was an acknowledged international expert on childhood TB and founder as well as honorary secretary of the Irish league.

In 1948, the Minister for Health, Noel Browne, appointed a national consultative council on tuberculosis chaired by Dorothy Price. This council took the decision to create a BCG committee and to proceed with mass vaccination. The headquarters of the national BCG committee was in St Ultan's clinic, and its first report in 1949 was explicit:

> *"The initiation of BCG vaccination will always be linked with the name of Dr Dorothy Price. Due to her conviction of the value of this preventative measure and to her individual endeavour sufficient clinical evidence was made available to her in her work in St Ultan's Hospital to warrant the adoption of BCG vaccination on a larger scale in Ireland."*[20]

Yet Dr Price's pioneering contribution to social medicine in Ireland was promptly forgotten. She died in 1954, from a stroke-related illness. After her death, her husband wrote a biography of her, printed for private circulation.[21]

Public health

Brigid Lyons was commissioned as an Army medical officer in 1922, and demobbed from the Army in January 1924. She was already a long-term patient in the Richmond Hospital, Dublin, having been diagnosed with pulmonary TB. President Cosgrave intervened and loaned her £200 – a substantial sum of money then, to be repaid from her military pension – from a fund set up to help people who had fallen ill as a result of war and military action. Lyons went to Nice to convalesce and there she met Captain Eddie Thornton, also an invalid. Following a sojourn in Switzerland, they returned to Ireland and married; Capt. Thornton subsequently left the Army and trained as first a barrister and later a solicitor.

Brigid Lyons Thornton, the first woman commissioned officer in the Irish Army, went on to a career in public health. Image: courtesy, Currach Press

After studying for a diploma in public health in UCD, Dr Lyons Thornton's first appointment was in Co Kildare, working on tuberculosis. But this was 1928 and she could fight the disease only with X-rays, malt, cod-liver oil, creosote and a sanatorium at Peamount, Co Dublin. After a brief appointment in Cork, she was appointed permanently to the Dublin Corporation Public Health Service, as a paediatrician in the Carnegie Centre in Lord Edward Street. She lectured to students of the diploma in public health, and her biographer Dr John Cowell recalls that "her impact was commonsense and practical and far exceeded that of many who paraded themselves as learned university professors." Lyons Thornton was active in the Royal Academy of Medicine in Ireland, serving as secretary to the public health section. On retirement, she became librarian to the Rotunda Hospital and also worked for the Medical Benevolent Fund, which helped impecunious doctors.

These three doctors are probably best known for their revolutionary activities, yet Ó hÓgartaigh argues that Lynn's most radical contribution was in medicine. She was a pioneering paediatrician whose neglect is part of a wider historiographical neglect of socio-medical history. Similarly, medical history has to date relegated Stopford Price to a footnote, yet she was, during her lifetime, an acknowledged international expert on childhood TB and widely cited worldwide.

Associated places:
Dr Kathleen Lynn: 37 Charlemont Street, formerly St Ultan's hospital; the Irish Medical Council headquarters, in Rathmines, Dublin, is named Kathleen Lynn house.
Dr Dorothy Price: 37 Charlemont Street (formerly St Ultan's hospital)
Brigid Lyons Thornton: Carnegie Centre, Lord Edward Street, Dublin, where she worked as a child-welfare paediatrician

Acknowledgements
The author is grateful to Dr Margaret Ó hÓgartaigh who read an early draft of this chapter. It should be noted that much of the information on Dr Lyons Thornton here is based on a memoir constructed by Dr John Cowell.

Anatomy of a Bog Body

Medical doctor Máire Delaney (1945-2002) combined her training in anatomy with her love of archaeology to become an
expert in bog body investigations. Her work provided vital clues
to the lives and deaths of the people whose bodies were found
preserved in peat. Her respect for the remains of our ancestors,
from both the recent and distant past, was something she also
instilled in her anatomy students.

by Anne Mac Lellan

"They look the same as us, you can see the eyes, the eyelashes, the beard stubble
... there's an immediacy you don't get from a skeleton. They are ancient yet no
different from us. They are better preserved than mummies and don't suffer from
the same element of shrinkage. It is fascinating to look at a person from 2,000
years ago and see their humanity." This is how Raghnall Ó Floinn, of the National
Museum of Ireland, explains our fascination with ancient bog bodies. For one
medical doctor, Máire Delaney, bog bodies were to become her professional
passion. She was one of the pioneers of the anatomical study of archaeological
human remains in Ireland, and left an important legacy that helped to shape
subsequent investigations.

In 2003, the year after Máire Delaney died, the bodies of two Iron Age men
were found in bogs in the Irish midlands. Both had been horrifically murdered.

The scientific, anatomical and archaeological investigations of the two bodies made international headlines, and are the subject of an exhibition at the National Museum of Ireland in Dublin, together with other Irish bog bodies and related finds. That exhibition, entitled Kingship and Sacrifice, is shocking in its detail: the man found at Oldcroghan, Co Offaly, had been stabbed, his nipples sliced, and holes cut in his upper arms through which a rope was threaded to restrain him, or pin him to the bog; he was also cut in half across the abdomen and beheaded. The man found at Clonycavan, Co Meath, received several axe blows to the head, and another to his chest and had been disembowelled. Oldcroghan man was tall – an estimated 6'3" – with manicured nails. Clonycavan man coiffed his hair high with a gel containing pine resin imported from Spain or France, possibly to make himself appear larger than his diminutive 5'2". The museum's Keeper of Antiquities, Ned Kelly, believes that these bodies were buried in the borders surrounding royal land or on tribal boundaries. "My belief is that these burials are offerings to the gods of fertility by kings to ensure a successful reign," Mr Kelly told BBC television's Timewatch programme, which explored the finds and the scientific and archaeological investigations.

The 'Irish bog body project' team assembled for the investigations comprised 35 specialists, including researchers from Ireland, Britain and Denmark. Osteo-archaeologist Máire Delaney, an expert in ancient remains, did not live to see these astonishing Iron Age finds, having died a year before they were discovered. Her absence from the analysis that engulfed these bodies, examining them from every possible scientific angle – Oldcroghan man's last meal was wheat and buttermilk, scars on his lungs showed that he had pleurisy – is summed up by Raghnall Ó Floinn: "[T]here was always an empty seat at the table . . . She would have been central to the work with her meticulous recording. She was very generous with her expertise."

Born in 1945, Máire was the granddaughter of that stalwart of Irish politics, former Irish Taoiseach and President Éamon de Valera. However, she rarely alluded to her connections to that most powerful of Irish political families. Indeed, when she was based in Northern Ireland for a time, the connection could have been a dangerous one. Máire's mother, Sally O'Doherty, was a nurse from Co Donegal, and her father, Prof Éamon de Valera, was a gynaecologist and a man who liked to sing Gilbert and Sullivan in the operating theatre. They met in the National Maternity Hospital, Holles Street, where they both worked. Perhaps unsurprisingly,

Máire opted to study medicine. Later, she is said to have regretted not choosing archaeology. Indeed, before she died, she had registered for a PhD in that subject but, due to her untimely illness, did not complete her thesis.

Máire went to school in St Louis's Rathmines, Dublin, and then to UCD. It was there that she met her first husband, Tom Delaney, who was studying English and archaeology. She took what has been described by her second husband and UCD contemporary Pat O'Connell as 'the scenic route' through college, taking a lively part in the drama society and pursuing her interest in archaeology, often to the detriment of her medical exam performance. During the summers, she excavated at the Neolithic burial ground in Knowth, Co Meath, under UCD archaeologist, Prof George Eogan, and in Inischaltra (Holy Island), Co Clare, alongside Liam de Paor, of UCD's department of modern history.

Some late prehistoric and early medieval burials were found at Knowth in the late 1960s and early 1970s and Maric applied her skills to them, although much of her early work on Knowth and Inishcaltra has not appeared in print. She was one of the few people then with anatomical and archaeological skills, according to Ó Floinn, who says her exposure to archaeology through both her husband and her uncle, Ruairí de Valera, a professor of archaeology, stood her in good stead. At the time, archaeologists tended merely to draw bones, record their presence and then send the bones to an anatomy department. The resulting report was often dry and sparse with, at most, details of age and sex and possibly some terse comments on pathological abnormalities. There was little appreciation of context or the importance of looking at bones *in situ*. Máire's aim was to research what could be inferred from the bones and their placement, to give the remains a context.

Tom Delaney and Máire married in 1972. That same year, Máire worked again on Inishcaltra with de Paor, where she examined exposed infant burials *in situ*. In each grave, a handful of quartz pebbles and a long stone pebble, sometimes a whetstone, sometimes a shaped stone of phallic appearance, were also interred. It was an opportunity to explore the context for the burials. When Tom was appointed to the Ulster Museum in Belfast, the couple moved north. His major undertaking there was to excavate the medieval quarter of Carrickfergus, Co Antrim, work that made him a noted Irish mediaeval expert. Meanwhile, Máire studied psychiatry at White Abbey, Belfast, but did not enjoy practising psychiatry, believing the approach was too heavily weighted in favour of drugs.

The couple had two children, Sarah and Aoife, but Tom Delaney died while they were still young, in 1979. He was just 32, yet he had made a major impact on Irish archaeology: *Keimelia*, a book published in his honour in 1988, acknowledged that the "recognition of the importance of urban archaeology in Northern Ireland was due in no small measure to [his] work . . . in Carrickfergus . . . .it is a measure of the esteem in which he was held in Carrickfergus that a public park containing part of the town wall is now named after him." Dr Tom Delaney is also immortalised by his friend, Nobel prize-winning poet, Seamus Heaney, as the dead archaeologist in *Station Island* (1984).

Máire remarried in 1984. Her second husband, Pat O'Connell, a widower with a daughter, Beatrice, had studied at UCD with Tom and Máire and, indeed, had previously helped to develop a computer program that allowed Máire to compute various formulae such as deducing height from bone length. This was unusual at a time when personal computers were in their infancy.

Human skeletal remains have been studied archaeologically in Ireland since the mid-19th century. From the 1960s to the early 1980s, however, few specialists were available to analyse archaeological human remains and many excavators appear to have sought the help of specialists in Britain. At best, remains found in Ireland were analysed by anatomists and medical doctors; at worst, they were reburied without analysis. When Maire Delaney delivered a paper at the 1974 meeting of the Organisation of Young Irish Archaeologists', one eminent professor admitted during the discussion to re-burying a corpus of 67 Iron Age/Early Christian burials at Knockea, Co Limerick, without analysis because he was unable to get expert assistance. In the 1980s Irish archaeologists began to seek specialist post-graduate training and to undertake research degrees in osteoarchaeology and palaeopathology and by 2002 there were over a dozen qualified osteoarchaeologists working within the island (Eileen M Murphy, writing in *Antiquity* in 2002).

Meanwhile, Máire Delaney was combining her passion for archaeology with her training in anatomy. From the mid-1980s, she became increasingly interested in what she called "the bones", says Pat O'Connell. She was doing some work for the National Museum on the human remains found at the Viking Wood Quay site in Dublin city, when she became involved with bog bodies and started to work with Raghnall Ó Floinn on the Meenybradden body.

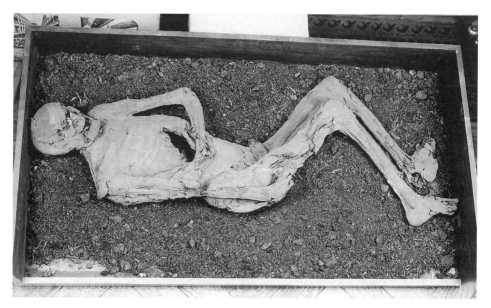

Gallagh man, found in 1821 near Castlebellew, Co Galway, and now in the National Museum of Ireland. Máire Delaney re-investigated the site at Gallagh where he had been killed some 2,000 years before. Image: © National Museum of Ireland

On May 3, 1978, farmer Frank Battles and his neighbours were hand-cutting turf at Meenybradden, Inver, Co Donegal when they discovered the remains of a woman wrapped in a woollen cloak and lying on her back. The cloak served as a shroud, and the woman was otherwise naked. There was no evidence of foul play and no associated artefacts. This 25-30 year-old woman was the first well-preserved bog body found in Ireland in the 20th century. Her remains were x-rayed, then stored in a freezer in Dublin, until 1985, when a full examination was begun.

Bogs are areas of soft, waterlogged land, usually containing large amounts of organic acids and aldehydes in layers of sphagnum moss and peat. This acidic and anaerobic environment often preserves the soft tissues of a cadaver even after the bones have dissolved away. Skin, eyes, intestines and hair may be so well preserved that the body appears almost modern. Bog bodies have been found across north-western Europe, their presence often associated with murder and ritual. They have been dated from Mesolithic to modern times, but the best-preserved come from the Iron Age and Roman periods. In Ireland, as many as 100 bog bodies have been found in both raised and blanket bog. Most of these are now 'paper bodies', preserved in records only. In Denmark, no new bodies have been found since the astonishing discoveries in the 1950s of the famous Tollund man and Grauballe man. So, the Meenybradden find in 1978 was significant.

Its examination in 1985 was prompted by the discovery of the Lindow bodies in England and the subsequent headline-catching investigation, which led to a new technique for preserving bog bodies. In 1983, police in Macclesfield, Cheshire, were investigating reports that Peter Reyn-Bardt had murdered his wife, Malika, 23 years earlier. Reyn-Bardt had boasted that he had killed, dismembered and buried her in his back yard. When workmen discovered a well-preserved skull, identified as a 30-50 year-old European woman, Reyn Bardt confessed to the murder. Just as the case went to trial, however, scientists at Oxford University came forward with a date for the skull: 1660 to 1820 years old. This was the first Lindow body. The following year, the body of a 2,000 year old Iron Age man was found in Lindow Moss peat bog. Dubbed 'Pete Marsh', the man had been brutally murdered or 'sacrificed': he had received three blows to his head, then been garrotted and had his throat slit.

To preserve 'Lindow man', the British Museum developed a new freeze-drying technique, which they offered to the Irish Museum for the Meenybradden body. But, as Ireland did not have freeze dying facilities then, the body was sent to the British Museum for preservation. Since the mid-1990s, however, the National Museum of Ireland has a state-of-the-art conservation facility at its Collins Barracks campus in Dublin, with walk-in fridges and freezers.

In 1995, the British Museum published a book about the investigations, *Bog Bodies: new discoveries and perspectives*, and Máire Delaney and Raghnall Ó Floinn contributed the chapter on Meenybradden woman. They concluded, however, that little could be learnt about either the cause of death or way of life, beyond the fact that: the woman was plump, there was no evidence of malnutrition, she had probably done some light manual work, and may have suffered from a lung and pleural infection. A radiocarbon date of AD 1570 was obtained from samples taken from one bone, although the woollen cloak's style dates somewhat earlier, to the Middle Ages. What was gleaned was a framework for future investigations, which the authors set out in some detail, including that the handling and description of a body be supervised by a specialist in human remains, and that it was important to coordinate investigations. "What Máire and I learned at Meenybraddan was used later . . . and it meant that the big discoveries made recently were not so daunting to deal with in terms of x-raying, tissue sampling, description etc," says Ó Floinn.

Maire Delaney now began to make contact with her peers in Britain, the Netherlands and Denmark, and to study bog bodies in earnest. She was particularly interested in techniques to find, record in context, analyse the findings and record them in a standard way. She re-investigated the site at Gallagh, Co Galway where a bog body was found in 1821. Gallagh man came to the Irish museum sometime in the 1850s, in a dried out condition, and naked except for a hooded deerskin cloak that extended to the waist and a rope around his neck in the form of a garrotte, reminiscent of the later Lindow man. Gallagh man was subsequently radiocarbon dated to 2,040 years old, putting him in the Iron Age. The site where he was found had not been preserved, but Máire returned to the location and, with the help of a local person, identified the site where Gallagh man had been pinned with wooden stakes into the bog, near Castlebellew in Co Galway.

In the early 1990s, Máire became a lecturer in anatomy at TCD. She enjoyed the teaching, and was a talented draftswoman, preparing many of her graphics herself. She was often called in by the then State pathologist, Dr John Harbison, to verify whether a body was an historical rather than a recent death. On one occasion, Pat O'Connell recalls her being called to Dundrum Castle, Dublin, where a skull had been found under a rose bush; the upper part of the face had been sawn off and was missing. Máire dated the skull to the 1920s, when a sausage factory operated in the area. She also worked on Bully's Acre, Dublin, when a traffic roundabout was being constructed on an area that had been used as a burial ground for victims of a 19th-century cholera epidemic.

In 2001, Máire Delaney was called on to identify the bodies of 10 IRA volunteers executed during the War of Independence. Tried and sentenced by military court martial, they were executed by hanging, between November 1920 and June 1921, and buried in unmarked plots in Dublin's Mountjoy prison. The first to be executed was Kevin Barry, an 18-year old medical student, whose death provoked a public outcry on account of his young age. The exhumation took a month and involved a team of archaeologists and the State pathologist. It had been feared that the men might have been buried in quicklime and that the bodies would have disintegrated, but Máire was able to identify them from prison records that included their height. She could also reassure their families that they were found intact, had not been tortured, and had been given a Christian burial. Following exhumation, the 10 volunteers were given State funerals and re-interred, with nine buried in Glasnevin Cemetery, Dublin, and one returned to Limerick.

Delany identified the exhumed remains of 10 volunteers executed during the War of Independence

Máire Delaney also assisted a group of young schoolgirls from the Dominican College, Belfast, on a project that earned them the top prize at the 1997 European Union Contest for Young Scientists in Milan. The three students studied stillborn pigs, which are biochemically similar to humans, and which they had buried for 10 months in a local peat bog. They found that the release of protein-degrading enzymes from a pig's liver peaks between 48 and 72 hours after death. As a result, a piglet buried three days after death was, 10 months later, little more than mush and bones, while another, buried three hours post-mortem, remained pink and well-preserved. Forensic entomologist Wayne Lord of the FBI Academy's child abduction and serial killer unit in Quantico, Virginia, is quoted in *Science* magazine, September 1997, as saying "From a forensic perspective, this work is unique. No-one

Tumbeagh, October 1998: the first bog body discovered in Ireland by an archaeologist, protected in a block of peat and ready to remove for preservation. Máire Delaney (left), Dr Wil Casparie and Dr Nóra Bermingham. Image: courtesy, Nóra Bermingham

has looked at bog environments in terms of human decomposition. The work may also interest archaeologists."

In 1998, when another bog body was found in Ireland at Tumbeagh, Co Offaly, Delaney was in a position to use the experience gained with the Meenybradden body. While the Meenybradden body travelled to the museum in the back of a car, the Tumbeagh body was the first bog body in Ireland to be removed and sent to the museum *in-situ* (blocked in peat) for analysis and conservation. The body was discovered in the late afternoon of September 17th, 1998, when a group of archaeologists working on an excavation noticed a small dark-brown leather-like flap exposed at the bog surface. Close by were yellow crumbs that looked like bog butter, a piece of wood, and a blackened bone. It was the first time an archaeologist had discovered a bog body in Ireland.

Wetlands archaeologist Nóra Bermingham recalls Máire's arrival at the site: "It was a moment of relief and, in truth, excitement, when she confirmed that the remains were indeed human." She adds: "In the bog, Máire always wore the same purple raincoat with hood pulled tightly around her face and the sleeves rolled up to her elbows so she could dig her hands in and really get to grips with the peat – this may sound strange to an outsider but, believe me, it's the only way of doing it. We worked very closely together on the project, developing strategies and discussing pros and cons of different approaches, probably *ad nauseum* and covering everything from the Pazaryk ice queens to Otzi [the Alpine Iceman found on a glacier in 1991] and the Egyptian mummies, until we were happy."

Bermingham and Delaney decided to hold off on conservation as long as possible, confident that keeping the remains in wet peat was a good approach to preserving the body in the interim. They worried that conservation would alter the composition of the remains and could produce false results with tests such as for trace metals and proteins. They held firm in the face of opposition and Nóra believes that their approach was justified.

Delaney and Bermingham jointly wrote a book on the Tumbeagh bog body (published in 2006 after Delaney's death); Máire concentrated on the anatomical and scientific testing, Nóra on the excavation and historical background. Máire drew on her experience of working with soft tissue remains (both earlier bog body finds and cadavers in her capacity as an anatomy lecturer) and skeletons recovered from archaeological sites. In Nóra Bermingham's estimation, her combined medical and archaeological background gave her the ideal experience to analyse bog bodies.

Everyone associated with Máire Delaney mentions her sense of humour. Ó Floinn says she was "an incredible mimic, iconoclastic, enjoying taking pompous people down a peg or two. She was anarchic, she lived life to the full." She was also interested in Irish culture, a regular attendee of the Willie Clancy summer school in traditional music, and a talented *sean-nós* (traditional 'old-style') singer. Interested in Donegal singers (her mother's home county), she started to locate out-of-print material, and a catalogue of her recordings has been lodged in UCD's School of Folklore.

The National Museum of Ireland's bog body exhibition includes only the Meenybraddan cloak, but not the body, on account of its relatively modern date. If Máire Delaney walked into the Kingship and Sacrifice exhibition today, she would surely be astonished by the Clonycavan and Oldcroghan bodies, but she would already be familiar with Gallagh man, whose resting place she rediscovered, and Baronstown man, whom she investigated.

Máire Delaney was not a high flyer on the international stage and her early death meant she did not achieve her full potential, but she left a legacy of careful investigation, meticulous note taking, attention to context and respect for the person – qualities to which any archaeologist might aspire. She was involved with the excavation and investigation of human remains from archaeological contexts for over 30 years, from the late 1960s until her death in 2002. She excavated human remains on sites including Knowth, Co Meath, High St. Dublin, Ballymacaward, Co Donegal, and Inishcaltra, Co Clare. She also reported on skeletal remains on numerous sites including Aughinish Island, Co Limerick, Marlinstown, Co Westmeath, Dublin Castle, and a large Early Christian cemetery in Rathfarnham, Co Dublin, as well as working on the Tumbeagh bog body.

Ó Floinn says: "She was sometimes insecure. She flowered late and tried to make sure she was doing whatever she did to the highest possible international standards." Her husband Pat O'Connell adds: "She disliked the sensational and she didn't like people being definitive without hard evidence." So, she did not make things easy for the documentary makers who included her in their programmes. Sadly, Máire Delaney died of cancer in 2002. She had self-diagnosed a melanoma in 1997, and was operated on, but five years later found a tumour in her breast and was dead within the year. Máire attributed the melanoma to a blistering hot day in Knowth in 1967 when she was badly burnt on the leg. Her widower, Pat O'Connell says: "One of the radiographers had been her student. They cried together until Máire advised her to remember she couldn't do the job unless she distanced herself from it. When do you ever give up teaching?"

The book that she and Nóra Bermingham wrote on the Tumbeagh body was her swan song, and she worked on the project well into her illness. Nóra says: "Máire and I agreed on so much – we both wanted to make sure we reached and set high standards and were keen to involve as many specialists, particularly home grown ones, as we could attract, and we were determined to get the work published… I must have received her final submission only two or three months before her illness progressed to such a stage that recovery was unlikely. It is only with hindsight that I realise how hard this must have been for her and her family as I didn't really understand how ill she was, she was always upbeat."

Acknowledgements

Thanks are due to: Pat O'Connell, Máire's widower, for an extensive interview and for commenting on the draft chapter; Dr Nóra Bermingham, wetland archaeologist, for her copious email correspondence from England, where she now lives, and for commenting on the draft; Dr Raghnall Ó Floinn, National Museum of Ireland, for a useful overview of the work on which he and Máire collaborated.

Carmel Humphries was an expert in insect identification with a photographic memory.
Image: courtesy, School of Biology and
Environmental Science, UCD

An Inspiring Zoologist

Prof Carmel Humphries (1909-86), the first woman professor of zoology at UCD, devised a technique for identifying small chironomid flies that is still used today. A big personality with a love of tiny insects, she was a famously entertaining teacher who inspired a generation of zoologists and was instrumental in opening up the field of freshwater ecology in Ireland.

by Seán Duke

The clouds of tiny 'dancing fly' frequently seen swarming over freshwater are the Chironomidae, also known as the non–biting midges. They are found on every continent, and their presence is used to assess water quality. Today, many can be identified from the microscopic skin (or exuviae) that the adult fly sheds when it emerges from the pupa, using a technique developed by Irish zoologist Dr Carmel Humphries. Pioneer of freshwater ecology studies, entertaining lecturer, formidable yet with a soft spot for staff and students . . . these descriptions of Carmel Humphries, professor of zoology at UCD for over two decades, from 1957 to 1979, will be familiar to anyone who had any contact with UCD's zoology department then. Humphries, an expert in insect identification, influenced a generation of Irish zoologists, and was instrumental in opening up the field of freshwater ecology in Ireland.

A native of Waterford, Carmel Humphries entered UCD in 1929, graduating in 1932 with honours in botany and zoology. She was a talented student who won several scholarships during her undergraduate days and a valuable postgraduate travel fellowship from the National University of Ireland which allowed her to study abroad after her degree. This meant she could choose where to further her studies, as nearly any laboratory, provided it has the space, will accept a well-qualified student who does not require support or funding.

Already interested in freshwater ecology, Carmel chose the laboratories of the Freshwater Biological Association at Wray Castle, Ambleside, on the shores of Lake Windermere in England's Lake District. This gave her the opportunity to work with some of the big names in freshwater ecology, among them Winifred Frost, T.T. Macan, and H.P. Moon. Here, she developed an interest in an unusual group of insects, the non-biting midges or Chironomidae (see panel), that are difficult to identify – what the experts would describe as "taxonomically challenging". They were the perfect subject for someone with her skills and talent, and especially her photographic memory, and they became her dominant research interest for the rest of her career.

"She really loved her early days in England, and it was there that her love of freshwater ecology developed," recalls Dr Edward J. Duke, now retired professor of zoology at UCD (and this author's father), who succeeded Humphries when she retired in 1979. Many of the chironomid species that Carmel had become interested in while working in the Lake District were hard to identify, and she realised she needed to improve her 'taxonomic' skills. Insect species in general can be difficult to identify, but the chironomids are notoriously so. However many species can be identified from the tiny cast-off skins, or exuviae, shed by the adults when they emerge from the pupal state. This makes chironomid identification a specialised and difficult field.

How better to train, than to work with the very best? So, after England, Carmel decided to pursue her research in Germany under August Thienemann, an international expert in insect taxonomy and ecology. In the 1920s, Thienemann had introduced the concept of feeding (or trophic) levels in a food chain. This concept, which ecology students will recognise, was based on the notion that the energy contained in food is transferred in an eco-system from the green plants (the 'producers') at the bottom up through several levels of 'consumers' (animals) and then back to the plants again.

Thienemann's laboratory at the Hydrobiologische Anstalt der Kaiser Wilhelm

The dancing chironomids

YOU KNOW them as the clouds of tiny 'dancing fly' or non-biting midge that swarm over lakes, rivers and shores, even if you do not know their scientific name, the Chironomidae. There are over 400 species in Ireland – a list continually extended by zoologists, with many more found in Britain and Europe – and ranging in size from 1mm to about 1cm. Fly-fishing anglers know them as 'duck fly', 'buzzers', and 'silver hawthorns', and use them as bait.

These two-winged insects spend most of their life as a larva in water – perhaps as much as a year – before metamorphosing into a pupa and then finally a fly. When the adult midges emerge from the pupal state, the cast-off skins, called exuviae, float on the water surface and become part of the flotsam, from where they can be scooped up with a net and examined under a microscope. Carmel Humphries pioneered this now widely used technique as a way of identifying chironomid species.

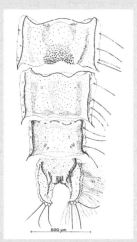

Chironomids are the only insect found on every continent, and their presence is used to assess water quality in lakes and rivers. Since the 1990s, scientists have also used larval capsules found in lake sediments as a measure of July temperature, allowing them to estimate summer temperatures as far back as the end of the last Ice Age. The midges are also commercially important, especially in Ireland, because they are one of the main foods eaten by game-fish such as trout and salmon. Some midge species contain high levels of a red blood pigment (hence their larvae are called bloodworms), which gives the fish flesh a nice pink colour. In recent years, the fish farm industry has developed feeds incorporating similar pigments to improve the appearance of farmed fish.

Drawing of part of the exuviae (enlarged) of a male midge of the species Zalutschia humphriesiae, *named after Carmel Humphries.* Image: courtesy, Declan Murray

Prof Carmel Humphries inspired a generation of Irish zoologists, including Dr Declan Murray, seen here in 1967. Murray and a UCD colleague Dr Colette Dowling later discovered a new species of non-biting midge which they named in Humphries's honour. Image: courtesy, Declan Murray

Gesellschaft was at Plön, in the Schleswig-Holstein region of northern Germany. It was by now well into the 1930s, yet in later years Carmel made no mention about the growing Nazi movement in Germany then, nor the threat of war. She was, it seems, more interested in her insect studies. When she later told colleagues how she enjoyed her time in Plön there was no reference to politics, the Nazis or Hitler. "She went to Germany just pre-war in the 1930s," said Prof Duke. "She never really talked about it in terms of it being a pre-war period, she just talked about the science, and the interactions, and the intellectual stimulation. In that sense she was somewhat apolitical."

At Plön Carmel had regular contact with Thienemann and other scientific leaders in both limnology (the biology of inland waters) and chironomid research, including F. Lenz, H. Uttermohl, W. Ohle and M. Goetghebuer. "It was a formative period in her career scientifically and probably character-wise as well, because she had a kind of Germanic attitude, I think, to science, in the sense that everything had to be in its own compartment," Prof Duke recalls. "While she could be sloppy with cigarettes [she was a heavy smoker], she wasn't sloppy when it came to the detail of doing her taxonomy and getting things into the right boxes."

At Thienemann's suggestion, Carmel Humphries began the first comprehensive study of the Chironomidae in Schleswig-Holstein's largest lake, the Grosser Plöner See, about 30 km² in area. This was based on collections of chironomid exuviae that she gathered from the lake, and it was now that she pioneered her main scientific achievement: using exuviae to identify the species present in a body of water. This technique is still widely used to determine both the species present and the water quality. Around the same time, Humphries and her Belgian colleague, Dr M. Goetghebuer, discovered a number of new chironomid species while working together. Carmel clearly developed a good personal and professional relationship with the famous Thienemann during this time. She had an almost photographic memory and an ability to recognise and remember special taxonomic features. This impressed Thienemann and was a skill she retained for many years.

Zoologist Dr Declan Murray is a former student of Humphries in whom she instilled a fascination with the Chironomidae. He specialised in these insects during his own career at UCD, and with his students identified over 330 chironomid species in Ireland, bringing the total number of these species known here to over 430. He recalls Carmel talking wistfully of her Plön days: "I remember Carmel sitting at the microscope with a cigarette in the corner of her mouth, talking about how she would row across the lake in the mists of early mornings, towing a plankton net behind the boat to skim the lake surface and collect exuviae of the insects which had emerged during the previous night. It was obvious that this was a formative period in Carmel's career, a time which she relished and spoke of with enthusiasm."

She would row across the lake in the dawn mist towing a plankton net to skim the surface and collect exuviae

After her years overseas, Carmel returned to Ireland in the 1940s and lectured for a number of years at University College Galway and Queen's University Belfast, before being appointed as an assistant in UCD's zoology department in 1947 in her late 30s. Assistant does not sound an impressive post, being the first rung on the ladder and below assistant lecturer, but jobs were hard to come by, and it was a full-time staff position. In fact, the key then was to get a foot in the door, and it was not unheard of for an assistant to be promoted straight to professor. At this point Humphries, who never married, moved to Rathmines, to a fine house opposite the St Louis Convent school.

A key moment in Carmel's scientific career was when she was awarded a D.Sc. degree in 1952. This is the highest scientific degree, and it is awarded by universities – in Britain and Ireland at least – for published work of very high quality. This achievement helped her to UCD's Chair of zoology five years later, in 1957. Carmel took over from Prof James Bayley-Butler, a noted inventor, and regarded by many as a genius and eccentric who could reputedly hypnotise frogs. Bayley-Butler had trained as a medical doctor and as a biologist, but opted to specialise in zoology, although his inventions included a process for canning vegetables, an anti-woodworm treatment, and a way to waterproof maps which he sold to the US military for the then sizeable sum of £5,000.

On taking over the department, Carmel introduced a number of changes. She initiated studies on Irish Chironomidae and began actively to direct post-graduate students in this area. She also encouraged research on the ecology and taxonomy of other freshwater species, and on Irish marine fauna. In the 1960s, when the zoology department moved from the Royal College of Science, on Dublin's Merrion Street (now Government Buildings, see Chapter 1) out to suburban Belfield, Carmel oversaw the move, and significantly she set up an active freshwater research (limnology) unit at the new Belfield location.

Carmel greatly enjoyed the teaching side of academic life. It was not unusual to hear foot stamping and cheering reverberate around the building during her lectures, in response to one of her witty biological quips. Carmel used the 'chalk and talk' method and, claiming that she was ambidextrous, would write with both hands. However, students recall that it was difficult to decipher what she had written on the blackboard no matter which hand she used, and that they were in real trouble on one occasion when she broke her right arm and wrote with her left. She also used an epidioscope, a forerunner of the overhead projector. Compared to today's teaching aids, this was a large, awkward piece of equipment but it allowed a lecturer to project a page of a book, for example, on to a big screen for students to see.

Carmel's lectures on evolutionary genetics were famous in UCD, particularly in the days before the 'sexual revolution' of the late 1960s and 1970s. The subject of sex inevitably came up in these, and engineering students often tried to sit in.

In the late 1950s, there was usually a group of nuns who were students and who typically sat in the front row of the theatre. Despite their presence, Carmel would calmly talk about the size of the sexual organ in some creature or other, and of what she termed "the Middlesex Regiment", those creatures, such as some fish, that have the ability to change sex. While Carmel was religious in her own way, and this was the 1950s, she did not hold back. Science was science, and that was it.

The genetics lecture would finish – pantomime like – with the human, and she would ask one of the laboratory attendants to bring in a human skeleton. In dramatic fashion she would announce: "Moore, bring in the skeleton." The side door of the lecture room would open, the unfortunate Mr Paddy Moore would trundle the skeleton in, and the students – keen to play their own part in the show – would gleefully stamp and shout: "Which one is Moore? Which one is Moore?" Every year this lecture ended up the same way, and Carmel seemed to enjoy the drama. The more the students stomped and shouted, the more she appeared to like it.

There were very few women in senior positions in Irish science in the post-War period, yet there were exceptions, including two other women professors at UCD – Dr Phyllis Clinch, professor of botany (see Chapter 10), and Dr Eva Philbin, professor of chemistry (see Ch. 11) – and Dr Máirín de Valera who was professor of botany at University College Galway (see page 131). Remarkably, when Carmel was appointed head of zoology in 1957, all five staff members in the department were women. The first man that Carmel appointed was Clive Kennedy in the early 1960s, followed by John Bracken in 1964, then Edward J Duke, and others followed.

For years, Carmel suffered with severe diabetes, a condition she kept private, although colleagues knew it could affect her, and sometimes leave her irritable, especially if she forgot to take her medication. Yet, she could also be extremely kind to her students, former students and junior members of staff, even acting as guarantor so one couple could buy their first home. Humphries was a diligent head of department, good at spotting a talented student, and encouraging them to further their studies, and she was known to read all of the theses that were submitted in zoology, even if the student's work was not in her own area.

UCD zoology students of the 1950s and '60s will fondly remember days spent

TELEPHONE NO. 61584

University College, Dublin

Zoological Department,

Upper Merrion Street, Dublin 2.

PROFESSOR C. F. HUMPHRIES, D.Sc.

27th November.......1964.

Mr Eammonn Duke,Ph.D.,
Department of Zoology,
Queens University,
Malone Road,
Belfast.

Dear Eammonn,

      Sorry to have missed you the other day when I could have given

my congratulations verbally. This is just a note to say how pleased I am

that you have got the Ph. D. I would suggest that you rest on your laurels

for a time before starting on your trip to the United States.

      Best wishes to Fiona. This is all for now.

      Yours sincerely,

      C.F.Humphries.

Letter congratulating Edward (Eamonn) Duke, who later succeeded Humphries as head of zoology at UCD, on his PhD. This was typical of her keen interest in the progress of her former students. Image: courtesy, Dr Edward J. Duke

with Carmel at the college's marine station in Coliemore Harbour, Dalkey, on the south side of Dublin Bay. The building was leased but, when an opportunity arose to establish a permanent station, the college turned it down, as Carmel felt that UCD should concentrate on freshwater studies and leave marine biology to UCG. Arguably, this was an opportunity missed as, to this day, UCD does not have a marine station, and is somewhat disadvantaged in this field of research.

Carmel was central to all the activities at the marine station, which entailed collecting material on Dalkey Island during the day and analysis later back at Coliemore. Students of this time fondly recall many amusing stories, and the general atmosphere of fun and learning which meant that they often worked late, until it was time to take the last bus back into the city and head home for the night. The Colimore station closed when UCD did not renew the lease, and though marine field trips continued to Sandycove and other parts of the Dublin coast, there was never the same sense of camaraderie as those halcyon days spent in Dalkey.

One of the most important legacies Carmel Humphries left is the generation of students she inspired, many of whom went on to achieve great things. Among them, John Hearn, now Provost of Sydney University, who was the first scientist to achieve artificial insemination with the panda bear, and whose work involved major collaboration with the Chinese authorities and their panda breeding programmes. Dr Tom Hayden is well known for his research on the deer heard in Dublin's Phoenix Park. Dr Jim Ryan went on to be a director of Bioresearch Ireland, a State initiative to commercialise Irish biotechnology research. Dr Martin O'Grady has been active for many years in efforts to stock Irish lakes and rivers and has been a senior advisor to government in this area.

Carmel's other great legacy was to further the scientific study of inland waters in Ireland, both freshwater and saline, namely limnology. Limnology at UCD really started with Carmel Humphries and she brought with her the expertise she gained from working with many of the top names in the field in England's Lake District and northern Germany during the 1930s and 1940s. She encouraged a succession of students to study limnology during her time and, though recent changes at UCD have altered the limnology unit, freshwater research still continues there.

As a fitting tribute to her, a newly discovered species of chironomid was named *Zalutschia humphriesiae* in her honour by two UCD zoologists, Dr Declan Murray and Dr Colette Dowling. And each year the Carmel Humphries prize, sponsored by Biotrin Technologies Ltd, is awarded for the best presentation at the postgraduate seminar day of UCD's School of Biology and Environmental Science.

Associated place:
11 Charleville Road, Rathmines, Dublin 6, her former home.

Acknowledgements
I would like to thank the former staff members from the UCD zoology department who provided information and personal remembrances, in particular Dr Declan Murray, retired senior lecturer; Dr Paddy Joyce, lecturer; Prof Edward J Duke, retired head of the department; also Dr Martin O'Grady, Central Fisheries Board.

Prof Phyllis Clinch (right), one of the most eminent
Irish botanists of the 20th century, photographed at
a UCD conferring in 1972. Renowned as a plant virologist,
she was also an excellent university administrator.
Image: Department of Botany, UCD

Queen of the Plant Viruses

Dublin-born botanist, Prof Phyllis Clinch (1901-84), made significant contributions to our understanding of plant viruses, especially viruses that attack the potato crop. Her work was of major agricultural importance at a crucial time in Ireland's economic development, and she is the only woman awarded a Boyle Medal for 'research of exceptional merit' since the prize was introduced in 1899. Her contemporary, Prof Máirín de Valera, an expert on seaweeds, was University College Galway's first professor of botany.

by Éanna Ní Lamhna

Potato, tomato and sugar beet growers owe a major debt of gratitude to a pioneering Irish botanist who, in the 1930s and '40s, investigated the viruses that can decimate commercial crops. By improving our understanding of viral diseases and how they are transmitted, Phyllis Clinch also paved the way for new disease-resistant crop varieties and effective procedures for controlling plant diseases. Her other achievements included being the one of the first women elected to the Royal Irish Academy and the first, and to date only, woman professor of botany at UCD.

Phyllis Clinch was born on September 12th, 1901, the fourth daughter of James Clinch and Mary Gabriel Powell. There were ten children born to the family but only five survived to adulthood: three died in infancy while two died as teenagers in 1919 from tuberculosis, leaving Phyllis as the second eldest of the surviving family. Phyllis's maternal grandfather was 'Major' Powell, reputedly the character on whom novelist James Joyce modelled Molly Bloom's father, Major Tweedy, in his novel *Ulysses*, and her mother was very friendly with the Joyce family: it used to amuse her greatly to hear little 'Jimmy Joyce', to whom she gave bread and butter with sugar on it as a treat, referred to as James Joyce.

The Clinch family lived in 'Mariae' on Leinster Road West in Rathmines, Dublin, and Phyllis attended the Loreto school on St. Stephen's Green. This progressive school taught science to girls in the early 1900s and Phyllis, liking the nun who taught chemistry, chose chemistry over history in her later years at school. When she left school in 1919 – there was no Leaving Certificate examination then – she opted to study science in University College Dublin (UCD), graduating with a first-class honours degree in chemistry and botany in 1923, gaining first place in her year and winning a post-graduate scholarship.

By 1924 she had gained an M.Sc degree by thesis and been awarded a research fellowship by Dublin County Council, already demonstrating her ability to make her mark in the world of botanical research. Next came a PhD on the metabolism of conifer leaves, under the supervision of UCD's newly-appointed professor of botany, Joseph Doyle. For this, Phyllis travelled to Imperial College, London, to research the biochemistry of the coniferales with Prof V. H. Blackman. Phyllis's research was of such a high standard that she published five papers jointly with Prof Doyle in two years, between 1926-28, and was awarded a PhD in 1928 as result of this work. Her first post-doctoral position was as assistant to the professor of botany in Galway, but before taking it up she was given an opportunity to study cytology (the structure and functions of cells), under Prof Alexandre Guilliermond in France. Guilliermond was one of the pioneering biologists studying the microscopic structures found in cells, and among the first to propose that the power-generating mitochondria were independent bodies that could replicate within a cell.

At the Sorbonne University, Phyllis quickly discovered that things were done differently in Paris. The Irish university working week then was five and a half days (a practice that continued to the 1970s), but not apparently in Paris. Except no one told Phyllis. By 1.15pm on her first Saturday she had become increasingly fidgety and was packing away her books when she drew the attention of the lecturer who referred exasperatedly to "*le English weekend*". The French were made of sterner stuff and Phyllis had to put in a full day on Saturday before being let go. Phyllis returned to Galway in late 1928 as a well-educated woman of 27 with impressive qualifications in chemistry, botany, plant physiology and now cytology. As it happened she was not to remain long in Galway, returning to Dublin the following year to join new and exciting research on plant viruses that was starting in the Albert Agricultural College, north of Dublin city, under Prof Paul A Murphy and Dr Robert Mc Kay.

In the late 1800s, a Russian biologist, Dimitri Ivanovsky, had done seminal work on the tobacco mosaic virus (TMV), which infects tobacco plants. He isolated the virus particles using fine porcelain filters, making it arguably the first virus to be discovered and the first time a virus was shown to cause disease. In the 'Albert' (now the location of Dublin City University), Ivanovsky's technique was being used in 1929 to study something very relevant to the Ireland of that time: virus diseases of potatoes. Phyllis Clinch had found her niche, and she was to work here on plant virus diseases for 20 years, until 1949 when she transferred to UCD's botany department as an assistant lecturer, the following year she was appointed to a lectureship.

Thanks to Phyllis Clinch, Ireland became the standard bearer for disease-free potato stocks

The virus research at the Albert College was of an internationally high standard and Phyllis earned a world-wide reputation as an expert in the field. Potato degeneration and disease had been a serious problem in Ireland up to this time, causing reduced crop yields and infecting seed potatoes. Phyllis tackled what was in effect a complex consisting of several viral diseases, and separated out the different viruses responsible. She looked at their effect on various potato cultivars or types, alone and in combination with each other. Most of these viruses were transmitted by insects, something that her colleague J. B. Loughnane elucidated. Significantly, however, Phyllis discovered that some varieties of potato were symptomless carriers of disease, and that these could transmit some viral infections. The Dept of Agriculture exploited these research findings to breed and propagate special stocks of disease-free potatoes that were made available to growers. In this way Ireland became the standard bearer for healthy seed potato stocks. The work was of huge economic importance at a time when, in the 1930s and '40s, Ireland was dependent on home-grown agricultural produce.

Phyllis Clinch published all this research in an Irish journal, the *Scientific Proceedings of the Royal Dublin Society*, in a series of nine papers between 1932 and 1949, some with J B Loughnane and P A Murphy. During this time she also published in the Dept of Agriculture's *Éire* Journal and in one of the most prestigious international scientific journals, *Nature*. In 1943 she was awarded a D.Sc. on the strength of her published body of work, the highest degree a scientist can be awarded.

Having cracked the enigma of potato diseases, Clinch turned her attention to tomato viruses, another area of commercial importance. Soon she had described in detail six viruses that cause diseases in tomatoes, and more scientific papers followed. Sugar beet was the next crop to receive her attention. Significantly, she now worked out how a particular group of viruses – virus yellows – were transmitted from one plant to another: as well as the expected method of transmission by insects that physically carried the disease-causing virus particles from one plant to the next, Phyllis discovered that the infection could also be transmitted through seed, and infect up to 40% of the resultant crop. It was the first time this method of transfer had been reported, and her work was queried by sceptical international plant pathologists. But Phyllis Clinch's research was impeccable and full confirmation of her finding was quickly forthcoming from the Netherlands. Now, grateful beet breeders could be added to the potato and tomato breeders already indebted to her.

Potato, tomato and beet breeders are all indebted to Phyllis Clinch

As the acknowledged Irish expert in the field of plant virus diseases, Dr Clinch was frequently called upon by puzzled officials in the Dept of Agriculture to identify plant diseases. They would forward specimens of diseased crops to her both to identify the causative agent and make recommendations for its control. Irish agriculture in the 1950s – long before the halcyon days of the EU's Common Agricultural Policy – owes her a great debt.

Recognition for her work was bestowed by the scientific community, especially in Ireland, and she was often the first person here to attain certain scientific

'For Research of Exceptional Merit'

IN 1899 the Royal Dublin Society (RDS) inaugurated a medal for scientific research of exceptional merit carried out in Ireland. Named after Robert Boyle (1627-91), who was born in Lismore, Co Waterford, and is internationally acknowledged as 'the father of modern chemistry', the medal was awarded to distinguished Irish scientists who published their work in the society's *Scientific Proceedings*.

The medal was first awarded in 1899 to physicist Prof George Johnston Stoney who, at an RDS lecture in 1891, first proposed the term 'electron' for the elementary particle. The Boyle Medal was not awarded every year – only when a suitable recipient was identified. Indeed, in the century to 1999 only 33 awards were made. Phyllis Clinch was the only woman, although male botanists featured large in the list.

On its centenary in 1999, the award was re-launched in association with *The Irish Times* in a new format. Today, the medal is awarded biennially, alternating between a scientist based in Ireland and an Irish scientist based abroad, for research that has attracted international acclaim. It comes with a bursary of €30,000 so the recipient can employ a researcher to further their research. The requirement to publish in the *Scientific Proceedings of the RDS* has been dropped (the journal itself ceased in 1980, to be replaced by the RIA's *Journal of Life Sciences*), and arguably the requirement to publish there had always limited the award. But the standards have not dropped: no award was made in 2007 because no suitable candidate was found.

The Boyle Medal.
Image: Courtesy, the RDS

honours. In 1949 she became one of the first women elected to membership of the Royal Irish Academy (RIA), along with mathematical physicist Sheila Tinney (assistant professor at UCD), and in the humanities Francoise Henry and Eleanor Knott. Clinch was characteristically modest: believing that the others merited membership, she marvelled that she was ever elected "with my diseased potatoes". She seems not to have commented on the fact that the academy, which had been in existence since 1787, was only then electing its first women members. Clinch went on to become a member of the RIA's council in 1973 and was a vice-president from 1975-77. In 1961 she was awarded the Boyle Medal by the Royal Dublin Society (RDS) for her scientific work and publications – the only woman yet to receive this medal (see panel). That same year, following a decade as a lecturer in UCD, she became the first woman professor of botany at the college, and indeed the only one so far, following the retirement of her former PhD supervisor, Prof Joe Doyle.

It was not a case of all work and no play for Phyllis Clinch. A keen bridge player and an even keener golfer, she was lady captain of her golf club in Dun Laoghaire in 1958, and her sideboard groaned with golf trophies. Clinch lived with her sister Birdie (Bernadette) at Lissarda, Granville Road, Foxrock, where Birdie kept house, in addition to having a career of her own. Phyllis was not in the least domesticated and could reputedly take two hours to make a cup of tea. Her interest was more in the outdoors than in the kitchen and she had a large well-kept garden. Nor was she greatly interested in material matters and drove the same Morris Minor for years, bequeathing it to her nephew Paul when she died. She was, however, deeply religious, and the daily rosary was never missed in her house.

Clinch was Professor of Botany at UCD from 1961-73, a period that saw the college begin transferring from Dublin city centre to the southern suburb of Belfield, a move spearheaded by the science faculty in 1964. It fell to Phyllis to move the botany department and to ensure a good share of the spoils in the new science buildings. Her excellent negotiating and management skills, and her friendship with the university's secretary and bursar, JP Mc Hale, did not hurt. The building allocated was to house the departments of zoology, geology and botany, and Phyllis managed to ensure a respectable share of the building, helped by the fact that botany attracted a large number of students under her professor-ship. The botany department acquired well-equipped teaching and research labs which supported its rapid growth and expansion into the 1970s, a testament to her administrative skills.

Galway, seaweeds and Irish

MÁIRÍN de Valera was the first professor of botany in University College Galway (UCG) and a gifted teacher. Instrumental in helping to rebuild European seaweed research in the years after World War II, she was appointed to UCG's then newly-created Chair of Botany in 1962, and held the post until she retired in 1977. Her own expertise was marine algae, and she published many scientific papers on this, particularly the seaweeds of Galway Bay.

Máirín de Valera (1912–84) was born in Dublin, the second child of former Irish President and Taoiseach, Éamon de Valera, and his wife Sinead. Like her counterpart Phyllis Clinch, she attended Loreto College, St Stephens Green, and studied science at UCD, graduating with a first class honours degree in botany. She stayed at UCD to research conifers with Prof Joe Doyle, again like Phyllis Clinch before her, earning both an MSc and, thanks to her excellent research, a travel scholarship. This allowed her to move to the University of Wales, Aberystwyth, where she switched to seaweed research. Next, she moved to Sweden, returning in 1939 to take up a post as assistant in UCG's department of natural history, as it was then called.

Máirín maintained her international contacts in the years after World War II, organising the first post-war International Phytogeographical Conference (the geographical distribution of plants), held in Ireland in 1949, and the first Seaweed Conference in UCG in 1950. Dedicated to Irish as an everyday language, Prof de Valera taught through both Irish and English. She was among the first women elected to the RIA, joining in 1956, and from then until her death in 1984 she served on several academy committees.

Prof Máirín de Valera: expert on seaweeds, and advocate of the Irish language.
Image: from the *Irish Naturalists' Journal*

Phyllis was professor of botany at the same time as Eva Philbin was professor of chemistry (see Chapter 11), and Carmel Humphries was professor of zoology (see Chapter 9). Two women biology professors in an era when these posts were practically all held by men, it might be thought that Phyllis and Carmel would be firm friends. The truth was that they had known each other from secondary school days and they always said that they were both the best of friends and the best of enemies! Although of comparable age and background, they had different leadership styles to say the least.

Clinch was a gentle lecturer. In those days, a technician sat through each lecture to work the slide projector. When Phyllis gave lectures on plant physiology to my class when in our fourth year, she had the after-lunch 'graveyard' slot from 2-3pm. There could be long intervals between one slide and the next and, in the warm lecture theatre and to the soporific sound of Phyllis's voice elucidating the intricacies of the dark reaction of photosynthesis, the technician would quietly fall asleep. "Next slide Joe", in the same tone, would elicit no response and Phyllis was always surprised that he had fallen asleep. Her efforts to waken him by raising her voice provided some of our amusement. Then, so taken was she with her topic that often the lecture ran on till 3.15pm and we did not dare shuffle our feet or rudely click our folders to indicate that the time was up. Instead, we had to wait until she would suddenly realise, "Oh, my goodness, it's a quarter past three!". Phyllis was a lady and, even as uncouth 1970s students, we recognised her as such. At the Christmas departmental party which she hosted every year, everyone was on their best behaviour, as she served genteel glasses of sherry and the most wonderful tangerines, still in their wooden box direct from Morocco. No wonder she was referred to by both staff and students – although not in her hearing – as "Auntie P".

Phyllis Clinch had the ability to recognise and encourage talent in her students, and great vision and aspirations for her department. She actively encouraged the development of cell biology, drawing on her own early experience in France. Her excellent understanding of plant diseases, acquired during her years in the Albert College, prompted her to expand the study of fungi (mycology) in her department. Younger colleagues were encouraged to study abroad and to achieve recognition in their fields. All of which contributed to the development of an active, broad-based school of graduate research. In particular she welcomed the expansion of phytosociology (the study of plant communities) when Fr. J.J. Moore SJ arrived. Indeed it was Moore who succeeded her as professor when, in 1973, she retired aged 72–50 years after she graduated from the same college in 1923.

There was no resting on her laurels when she retired. She became more active in the Royal Irish Academy, was elected a vice-president of the RDS in 1977, and a member of the board of visitors to the National Museum of Ireland. She continued to garden, to play golf and bridge, and to potter about in her ageing Morris Minor. On October 19th, 1984, she died suddenly while on holiday in Tenerife, and is buried in the family plot in Mount Argus cemetery, Harold's Cross, Dublin. A somewhat reserved and conventional woman, Phyllis Clinch left an indelible mark on botanical studies in Ireland.

Associated places

'Mariae', Leinster Road West, Rathmines, Dublin, and Lissarda, Granville Road, Foxrock, Co Dublin.

Acknowledgements

I wish to acknowledge the help given to me by Paul Clinch, Mary Stuart, Charles Mollan, Jim White, Hubert Fuller, Sheila Macken, Margaret Finlay, Mary Kelleher, Gerard Whelan and Ester Murnane.

Dr Eva Philbin: an expert in the chemistry of the flavonoid compounds found in plants, she was the first woman professor of chemistry in Ireland. Image: courtesy, the Royal Irish Academy.

The Doyenne
of Irish Chemistry

Mayo-born chemist Eva Philbin (1914-2005) combined academic excellence with a warm humanity and unmistakable integrity. She specialised in the complex chemistry of important biological compounds, and made a lasting contribution to Ireland's pharmaceutical and chemical industry. She was a foundation member and fellow of the Institute of Chemistry and was its first female President, at a time when the profession was still predominantly male.

'In questions of Science the authority of a thousand is not worth the humble reasoning of a single individual.'

Arago's Eulogy of Laplace

by Prof Dervilla M X Donnelly

The health benefits of green tea and red wine, dark chocolate and citrus fruits are due in large part to the flavonoids they contain. Over 5,000 different flavonoids are known, and they are found across the plant kingdom. Some are responsible for the colours of flowers, others help plants to fight off insect attacks, although we still don't understand the function of many flavonoids. Their health benefits are thought to be due to the fact that some flavonoids trigger antioxidant activity, helping to fight cancer and cardiovascular disease, as well as allergies and inflammation. Not surprisingly, there is considerable scientific, medical and pharmaceutical interest in these compounds and their complex chemistry, in understanding their function and especially finding ways to synthesise them in the laboratory. One Irish chemist, Eva Philbin (née Ryder), made flavonoids her life's work, and paved the way for a deeper understanding of their biological function and their potential for use as pharmaceuticals.

Eva Maria Philbin was born on January 4th 1914, the first daughter of George and Kate Ryder in Ballina, Co Mayo. Eva's mother, described as the 'one of the greatest business women in the west', had a general store and bar by the River Moy, while her father was a quiet man who loved to read poetry and contemplate life. Eva, along with her only sibling Rita, attended the local convent school winning a scholarship to University College Galway (UCG), where she earned a first class honours B.Sc. She followed this with an M.Sc in 1937, researching carbohydrate chemistry and in particular identifying the sugars found in seaweeds. This study was under the direction of a colourful and able chemist, Prof Thomas Dillon, a brother–in–law of Joseph Mary Plunkett, one of the executed 1916 leaders and a signatory of the Proclamation of the Irish Republic. Dillon himself had close ties with the Irish independence movement and advised Sinn Féin on the manufacture of explosives. He was arrested in 1918 and interned in Gloucester Prison. It was while a 'guest of his majesty's government' that Dillon was appointed to UCG's chair of chemistry. Later, as students at University College Dublin (UCD), we enjoyed hearing at first hand from Eva the details of this outgoing and clever chemist and it was evident how much she respected his scientific achievements and colourful personality.

On completing her M.Sc. thesis, Eva was appointed as an assistant in UCG's chemistry department. Two years later, at the start of World War II, she switched to industry, becoming chief chemist with two Galway-based chemical companies: Cold Chon Ltd, which to this day makes road surfacing materials and bituminous binders, and Hygeia Ltd (a company within the same group) which still makes chemical products for farms and gardens. Both companies were set up in the 1930s by a pioneering industrialist, Dr Donny Coyle. Wartime restrictions, however, meant that the companies no longer had access to their usual raw materials, and Eva successfully developed and sourced alternatives, demonstrating an ability to make her mark in the world of industry. At this time she met and married John Madden Philbin, an accountant and secretary of the Irish Glass Bottle Co, and they had two daughters Eimer (Philbin-Bowman) and Deirdre (Philbin-Dargan), and a son Liam.

In 1945 Eva joined UCD's chemistry department where she was successively demonstrator, assistant lecturer and college lecturer over a period of years. These were difficult times for the universities and especially science departments, Eva, in collaboration with the late Prof T.S (Tom) Wheeler, set about developing an active research school in 'natural product chemistry', focusing

Eva (left) and her younger sister Rita, with their father George and mother Kate, described as 'one of the greatest business women in the west of Ireland'. Image: courtesy, the Philbin family

on the flavonoids. These plant compounds have what chemists describe as a basic 15-carbon atom structure arranged in two benzene rings joined through a three-carbon oxygen heterocylic ring. Spatially, the atoms on the oxygen heterocylic ring can be arranged in different three-dimensional ways, which gives them a complex stereochemistry. Manufacture is also difficult as the different atomic arrangements can have different biological and chemical properties, despite having the same chemical composition. For her PhD, Eva studied flavonoid chemical reactions, notably the Wesley-Moser rearrangement and the Baker-Venkataraman transformation, and published the first of a series of scientific papers on this subject in 1952 in the journal *Chemistry and Industry*.

Shortly after receiving her doctorate, Eva travelled to Zurich to the organic chemistry laboratories at the Eidgenossische Technische Hochschule (ETH) to study under the famous Prof Vlado Prelog, and it was here that she became interested

Eva Philbin and her husband Jack: Eva placed great importance on family life, and found time for astronomy and Cordon Bleu cookery. Image: courtesy, the Philbin family

in the stereochemistry of flavonoids. She later described Prelog as a man of great intelligence, blessed with a great memory, who always seemed to be the centre of conversation, surrounded by the high-calibre scientists who were attracted to his laboratory, yet modest, unselfish and generous to a fault. This short stay in Zurich yielded a joint publication with Prelog in a Swiss journal (*Helvetica Chim Acta*, 1956), an indication of her natural skill and ability. This was the first of numerous scientific publications by Eva and her many collaborators on flavonoid stereochemistry. The award of a DSc degree in 1958 was further testimony to the value of her work.

With Prof Wheeler's untimely death in 1962, Eva took over the headship of UCD's chemistry department, one of the largest departments in the college. She led with great success, showing resolve where necessary and genuine understanding of staff concerns. Very quickly she was called on to supervise the move from the College of Science in Merrion Street, Dublin city, to new laboratories at Belfield, in suburban south Dublin in 1964. These new laboratories were part of one of the largest building projects then undertaken in the Irish Republic. Eva pursued a policy of developing the various branches of chemistry, both physical and inorganic, and attracting graduates from other countries, giving the department an international flavour and academic excellence it retains to this day.

UCD's chair of chemistry has a complex lineage, with origins in both the Royal Dublin Society (RDS) and the Catholic University. The RDS established its chair in 1796, and for the first 58 years the position was held by two internationally famous scientists: Irishman William Higgins FRS, and English chemist Edmund Davy FRS. In 1854 the chair was transferred to the Museum of Irish Industry (MII, see chapter 1) where it remained until 1867, when it was transferred to the then newly-established Royal College of Science. Meanwhile, a second chair of chemistry was established in the Catholic University School of Medicine (founded in 1855), which was moved in 1879 to University College Dublin. Finally, in 1926, the two chemistry chairs were united with the transfer of the Royal College of Science chair to UCD (then a constituent college of the National University of Ireland). The professorship was subsequently held by Hugh Ryan, Thomas Nolan and then Tom Wheeler, all international figures in their own right. Eva was the first woman to hold the chair, of which she was immensely proud.

It was Prof Hugh Ryan who began researching flavonoid pigments at UCD, work that has now been carried through many generations. Flavonoids are both important and interesting and, from a research point of view, scientifically challenging. The studies at UCD have attracted a wide range of chemists and biologists investigating flavonoid occurrence, distribution and biological function, how to synthesise them in the laboratory, and even how they interact with mammalian cells and tissues.

Returning from Zurich, Eva began a study with Tom Wheeler on the subtle and elusive stereochemistry of a particular subgroup, flavan-3, 4-diols (see diagram page 140). This required the use of the then new technique of nuclear magnetic resonance imaging (NMR) and, as there was no NMR facility in Ireland until 1969, the UCD team collaborated with Prof E.J.Corey of Harvard University, and used its facility; the results were published in a joint paper with Corey. In 1955 Wheeler and Philbin were instrumental in hosting an international symposium at UCD on 'recent advances in the chemistry of naturally occurring

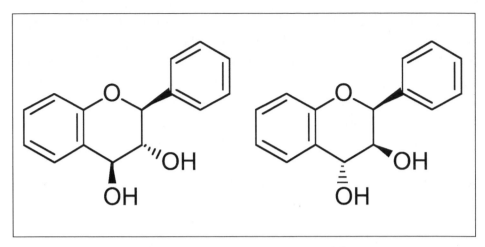

Two stereoisomers (having the same chemical composition, but different atomic arrangements) of the flavonoid trans-flavan-3,4-diol *which Eva Philbin studied.*

pyrones' to mark the 40th anniversary of Hugh Ryan's first paper on flavonoids.

The Dublin laboratories had an international and, in today's language, a 'world class' status, with numerous publications in international journals. The department's many postgraduate students formed the basis of Ireland's chemical and pharmaceutical industry, where Eva exerted a beneficial influence both academically and personally Visit the department's 'common room' and you will proudly be shown the signatures on the wall of famous chemists such as Nobel laureates R.B. Woodward and Derek Barton, to name but a few. Prof Woodward, of Harvard University, who was then arguably the world's most outstanding organic chemist, visited in 1967 to give the inaugural Wheeler lecture, a series Eva initiated in memory of her predecessor. UCD's large lecture theatre was filled to overflowing and the remaining students had to be satisfied with a relayed version in the adjacent theatre. The lecture lasted two hours, and chalk and blackboard were the order of the day.

The important work on the flavonoids continued under Prof Philbin's direction until her retirement. Slowly, her research team amassed valuable information on how to synthesise these chemicals. The resurgence of interest in drugs based on natural compounds has rekindled interest in the flavonoids and their potential as antioxidants, enzyme inhibitors, pigments and light screens.

Eva's work was recognised by the scientific community, especially in Ireland. She was elected a science member of the Royal Irish Academy in 1957 and for many years was an active council member, and vice-president 1970–1971 and senior vice-president in 1980. When a bicentennial history of the RIA was published in 1985, Eva was invited to write the chapter on chemistry. The preceding year she had written an account of the life and work of one of the most eminent chemists of the 18th century, Galway-born Richard Kirwan (1733–1812). In 1989, on the occasion of her 75th birthday, the academy dedicated a *festschrift* to her. No fewer than 115 authors contributed, reflecting her popularity with her many students, co-workers and colleagues.

UCD's science faculty in the 1960s was unusual, as three of the professorial chairs were held by women: Carmel Humphries in zoology (see chapter 9), Phyllis Clinch in botany (see chapter 10), and Eva Philbin in chemistry. These three women had very different personalities but all were noted for their academic excellence and kindness and consideration for staff and students. Eva was an inspiration to generations of science students, particularly women students. Today she would be described as a 'role model', an expression she would have found amusing, though gender discrimination was rampant in those years. At that time, for example, the children of male staff did not have to pay tuition fees, but because Eva was a woman her daughters Eimer and Deirdre were not eligible for this generous facility.

Eva combined her academic gifts with integrity, and she showed genuine kindness to staff and students, ready to listen to their concerns whether academic or personal. They always found a sympathetic and wise friend in her and in turn were influenced by her caring attitude. Her love of chemistry was infectious and this she passed on to many. She enjoyed playing with words and this stood her in good stead when results had to be put on paper either for a thesis or a publication. Many a graduate learned a lesson that stood in good stead when they had to write reports later in life.

Eva was an outstanding head of department, whose charm, ready sense of humour and patience made her a unifying influence: we were a team, and the odd insurrection went nowhere thanks to her ability to diffuse a situation and find an amicable solution. Graduates were always welcome in the department and Eva, helpful and supportive, knew the history of each individual who had passed through her hands. She was a strong supporter of her profession and was a foundation member and Fellow of the Institute of Chemistry of Ireland, established in 1950, and in 1966 Eva became the institute's first woman president, reflecting the esteem in which she was held. She was also an active member of the Irish branch of the Royal Institute of Chemistry and a Fellow of the Royal Society of Chemistry. Among her many public duties was membership of the first National Science Council and the Nuclear Energy Board.

It was not a case of all work, and Eva pursued many other interests with tremendous energy. She was a Cordon Bleu cook and, like her father, had a great love of poetry. You could find her happily reading a poem while watching an experiment refluxing in the laboratory. Another fascination was astronomy and later in life she invested in a telescope and would regale us with her observations over coffee next morning, more often than not providing with some delicacy which she had cooked that morning. It was a delight and privilege to have counted her as a true friend.

Despite the demands of her career Eva placed tremendous importance on family life. She and Jack were devoted to each other and to their children. To their sorrow, their only son Liam was severely handicapped: one of Eva's practical responses to this challenge was to become a founder member of a parent-friends support group for the mentally-handicapped. When this association was later merged with other groups it became the National Association for the Mentally-Handicapped of Ireland. Eva and Jack continued their active involvement in the association well into their retirement. Their daughters Eimer and Deirdre are members of the medical profession and both are in practice in Dublin. Jack predeceased Eva in 1997.

Associated places

33 Nutley Road, Dublin 4: the Philbin family home

Acknowledgements

I wish to acknowledge the help given to me by Eimer Philbin-Bowman, Deirdre Philbin–Dargan, David Brown, Charles Mollan, Mary Kelleher and Sara Whelan.

Dame Kathleen Lonsdale, FRS:
'She appeared to own the whole
of crystallography in her time.'
Image: courtesy, The Irish Times

The Stuff of Diamonds

X-ray crystallographer, professor, peace activist and prison visitor ... Dame Kathleen Lonsdale (1903- 71), from Newbridge, Co Kildare, achieved many firsts and even had a form of diamond named in her honour.

'Very few have made so many important advances in so many different directions.'

Dictionary of Scientific Biography

by Dr Peter Childs and Anne Mac Lellan

World-class physicist, crystallographer, Baptist turned Quaker, chemistry professor, peace activist, one of the first two women elected as Fellows of the prestigious Royal Society in London, prisoner, first woman professor at University College London, Dame of the British Empire. . . Hard to believe that Professor Dame Kathleen Lonsdale FRS was the daughter of an Irish postmaster.

Kathleen Lonsdale (née Yardley) was born to Harry Yardley and Jessie Cameron in Newbridge, Co Kildare, in 1903. Yardley had been a regimental sergeant major at the nearby Curragh army camp, turned postmaster, with a staff of six sorting mail for the English troops. His wife Jesse Cameron was a diminutive Scottish woman, who owed her short stature to childhood rickets. Kathleen, referring to her position in the family as the tenth and final child, later wrote: "Perhaps, for my sake, it was as well that there was no testimony against a high birth rate in those days."[1]

Kathleen's earliest Irish memories include attending Church of Ireland services and the Methodist Sunday School in Newbridge, and learning to count with yellow balls in the local school. Her father was widely read, enjoying books he picked up from junk stalls on subjects as diverse as the antiquities of Peru and the birds of Western Australia. He especially enjoyed encyclopaedias. Later, Kathleen said of her father, who died when she was 20: "I think he was fond of us and did not know how to show it. I wish I could have been fonder of him. I think it was from him that I inherited my passion for facts." However, drink and irritability drove her parents apart. In 1908, Kathleen's mother, who was a member of the strict Christian Baptist persuasion, left him and brought the children to Seven Kings, Essex, in England.

From then until 1914, Kathleen attended the local Downshall Elementary School, winning a scholarship to Ilford County High School for Girls. A good student, especially in mathematics and science, she had to attend classes in physics, chemistry and mathematics at the Boy's High School, as her school did not offer these subjects. In addition to her academic pursuits, she enjoyed gymnastics, games and country walks with friends. Unfortunately, her older siblings were not so lucky in their education: financial constraints meant they could not stay on at school but had to work to support the family. However, her brother Fred Yardley did manage to carve out a career: he become an early wireless operator, and is remembered as the operator who received the last distress signals from *RMS Titanic* in 1912.

Kathleen excelled in her exams, winning a 'county major scholarship' with distinctions in six subjects, and she was allowed to enter Bedford College, part of the University of London, at the relatively young age of 16. First she read mathematics then, at the end of her first year switched to physics, against the advice of her old headmistress, who warned that she would never distinguish herself in that subject. Perhaps these words acted as a spur? For in 1922, Kathleen came top in the University of London B.Sc. examination, with the highest marks in ten years. As a result, the Nobel physicist Prof William Bragg, one of her examiners and a pioneer of X-ray diffraction, invited her to join his prestigious research school at University College, London (see Panel).

W.H. Bragg was an exceptional supervisor, and Kathleen wrote: "He inspired me with his own love of pure science and with his enthusiastic spirit of enquiry

Crystal Structures

X-RAYS can be used not just to see inside a body, but also to reveal the molecular structure of crystals. Crystallography, the study of crystal structure, arguably starts with the work of mineralogist René-Just Haüy (1743-1822), but it really began as a science in 1912, when Max von Laue showed that X-rays, discovered in 1895, could be used to look inside crystals. William and Lawrence Bragg, father and son, then used X-rays to solve simple inorganic structures and developed Bragg's Law to explain X-ray scattering in crystals, known as diffraction patterns. In 1915, they were jointly awarded the Nobel prize for physics.[2] World War I disrupted the research, but "after the war, the Braggs divided the crystal world between them. The father, at University College, London, chose the organic structures and quartz, and his son, at the University of Manchester, took the rest of the inorganic substances."[3]

and at the same time left me entirely free to follow my own line of research." On Bragg's advice, Kathleen worked on the structure of simple organic crystals, and collaborated with W.T. Astbury on the theory of X-ray diffraction. In 1923, W.H. Bragg moved to the Royal Institution in London and Kathleen went with him. There, Bragg set up a team of bright young international researchers, including another Irish-born crystallographer, John Desmond Bernal (1901-71, from Nenagh, Co Tipperary,). Unsurprisingly, in an era when women scientists were a rarity, Kathleen was the only woman in this early group.

In 1924 Kathleen and Astbury published a landmark paper on 'Tabulated data for the examination of the 230 space-groups by homogenous X-rays' in the Royal Society's *Philosophical Transactions*, just two years after her graduation. In the following years, international crystallographers recognised the need for more comprehensive tables for crystal structure determination, and Kathleen joined the editorial group concerned with the production of new tables, and provided the structure factor formulae for each space group. The resulting *International Tables*, published in 1935, were only the beginning of a project to which she devoted much time and energy during her subsequent career.[4]

While in London, Kathleen met Thomas Lonsdale, an engineering student at University College. They married in 1927 and moved to Leeds when Thomas got a job in the Silk Research Association. Thomas was to prove an ideal husband for a woman scientist: at a time when many men would have expected their wives to stay at home and pursue a more domestic career, he encouraged Kathleen to continue her scientific work and research. He had not married to get a free housekeeper, he declared. In one of her many writings, Kathleen later wrote her prescription for career-minded women, who also wanted to marry:

> For a woman, and especially a married woman with children, to become a first-class scientist she must first of all choose, or have chosen, the right husband. He must recognise her problems and be willing to share them. If he is really domesticated, so much the better. Then, she must be a good organiser and be pretty ruthless in keeping to her schedule, no matter if the heavens fall. She must be able to do with very little sleep, because her working day will be at least twice as long as the average trade unionist. She must go against all her early training and not care if she is regarded as a little peculiar." [5]

Kathleen may, indeed have appeared a little peculiar. Dorothy Hodgkin, her friend and colleague and later Nobel laureate, described her as "short, with very fuzzy hair usually cut for her at home by Thomas. She had rather little time or money to spend on clothes, but she was fond of lovely things and liked to be nicely dressed for occasions." For her investiture as a DBE at Buckingham Palace, Kathleen was to make herself a small hat using lace, coloured cardboard and nine-pence worth of ribbons.

'For a married woman with children to become a first-class scientist she must first choose the right husband'

While in Leeds, Kathleen Lonsdale worked on X-ray diffraction in the university's department of physics. In what would prove a seminal opportunity, Prof C.K. Ingold in the chemistry department gave her some crystals of hexamethylbenzene to study. This was the first and most important structure Kathleen solved correctly, according to Hodgkin: Lonsdale showed conclusively that the benzene ring was flat, something that chemists had been arguing about for 60 years. Her discovery

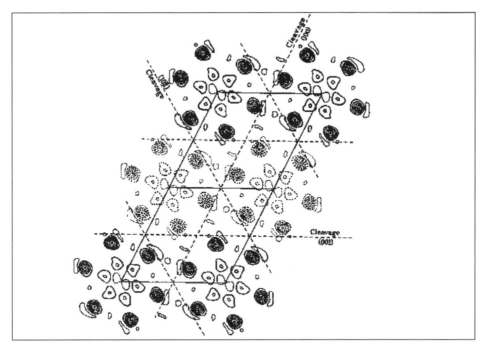

Lonsdale's landmark Fourier synthesis map of hexachlorobenzene. Her analysis revealed that benzene's ring is flat. Source: *Proc. Royal Society of London,* Series A. Vol. 133 No. 822, 1931. p 546 fig 6.

was a major milestone in organic chemistry. Lonsdale also applied Fourier analysis for the first time to analyse X-ray patterns in solving the structure of hexa-chlorobenzene (see Figure).[6]

Meanwhile, at home in the evenings, Thomas conducted experiments in the kitchen for his PhD, while Kathleen did X-ray diffraction calculations by hand – in the absence of computers, this was a complex and tedious process. In 1929, their first child Jane was born and, soon afterwards, they returned to London, where two further children, Nancy (1931) and Stephen (1934) arrived. The move and the children disrupted her experimental work again and she stayed at home. In 1931, Sir William Bragg wrote to her: "A piece of good news! Sir Robert Mond is giving me £200 with which you are to get assistance at home to enable you to come and work here. Can you come and see me soon?" Childcare costs were an issue then as now, and this funding enabled her return to research at the Royal Institution with Bragg. She stayed there for 15 years – for a time, occupying Michael Faraday's old room – and worked on many areas related to X-ray crystallography, both theoretical and experimental. In 1936, she was awarded a D.Sc. by University College, London.

Kathleen Lonsdale's critical abilities were not confined to the laboratory, and she went on to take an active role in a number of social causes. As an adult, she found the beliefs of the Baptists (her childhood faith) restrictive, and with her husband she joined the Religious Society of Friends, or Quakers, attracted by their advocacy of nonviolence and pacifist action; she was also vegetarian. Her opposition to war began during World War I when her home was on a Zeppelin route. She remembered doing her homework with a candle under the dining room table and once, when a Zeppelin was shot down, her mother burst into tears. The children looked on in amazement – after all, the Zeppelin crew was German – but Mrs Yardley explained that, for all that, they were just boys, and Kathleen began to wonder if war was ever justified.

So, at the start of World War II, when everyone in Britain was expected to register for war service, Kathleen deliberately ignored the requests. She was summonsed and fined £2 for failing to register, but refused to pay the fine and was sent to Holloway Prison for one month. While in prison, she wore prison uniform and had to clean floors and do other menial tasks. She was allowed books and papers, however, and managed to do seven hours scientific work each day. Her husband Thomas later said that going to prison was the single most formative experience in Kathleen's career. Lonsdale got on well with most of the prisoners and some of the officers, and liked to recall one prisoner advising her not to leave anything around as "there are thieves, dearie, even in here." Her brief sojourn in prison marked the start of a life-long interest in prison reform and she became a prison visitor for several women's prisons.

'Going to prison was the single most formative experience in her career'

In 1945, Kathleen Lonsdale and a biologist, Marjorie Stephenson, were elected as Fellows of the Royal Society in London, the first women elected to FRS since the society's foundation nearly 300 years before. Established in 1660, the Royal Society is one of the world's oldest and most famous scientific institutions, and election to fellowship is regarded as one of the top distinctions a scientist can achieve. Kathleen was now encouraged to move into academic life and, in 1946, she became a 'reader' (associate professor) in crystallography at University College, London. Three years later, she was appointed professor of chemistry – the first woman professor in the University's history – and head of the crystallography department. Only then, at the age of 43, did she start to build her own research group and become involved in teaching. However, Hodgkin notes that Kathleen's university lectures were regarded by many of her students as difficult, even incomprehensible. "She was a little impatient with those who could not follow her line of thought, forgetting perhaps that, though she might feel herself inadequately trained, her mathematical back-

C. J. Varney

The author of this pamphlet
KATHLEEN LONSDALE
is a Doctor of Science and graduated from London University in 1922, with first-class honours in physics. She at once began—and still continues—to do full-time research work in pure science. She was married in 1927 and obtained her degree as a D.Sc. in 1929. She has become well-known in the international scientific world for her studies. She joined the Society of Friends (Quakers) in 1935. Her principal interests are in education and penal reform. In March 1945 she was made a Fellow of the Royal Society—one of the few women to be so honoured.

Kathleen Lonsdale published an account of her stay in prison as a conscientious objector. Prison was, she said, the single most formative experience of her career. Image: courtesy, Charles Mollan

ground was much more solid than that of most chemistry students." Yet, Kathleen also guided many beginners through their early researches and her general lectures were often "a joy to listen to, easy to follow and brightened by stories and illustrations."

Kathleen Lonsdale worked in X-ray crystallography for half a century: from 1922, when she started as a young research student, to her death in 1971. Her published papers stretch from that first landmark paper in 1924 to her last one, published posthumously in 1972. She trained many students in the techniques and made contributions in many areas, and was the first woman elected president of the International Union of Crystallography (1966). Hodgkin summed up her contribution to science when she wrote: "There is a sense in which she appeared to own the whole of crystallography in her time."[7]

Amongst her many significant scientific contributions, she established the long-disputed structure of benzene and showed that it was flat (planar) and symmetrical. Prof C.K. Ingold wrote of this paper: "Ever so many thanks for your wonderful paper on hexachlorobenzene. The calculations must have been dreadful but one paper like this brings more certainty into organic chemistry than generations of activity by us professionals." Lonsdale was the first to apply Fourier methods to solving organic structures, showed that sigma and pi electrons existed in benzene, and provided experimental evidence for the molecular orbital theory of atomic structure. She helped to establish the theoretical basis of structure analysis by drawing up structure factor tables (with W.T. Astbury) and then editing the *International Tables of X-Ray Crystallography*, the crystallographer's bible, and did important work on thermal motion and diffuse scattering in crystals.

Lonsdale also made important investigations into natural and synthetic diamonds and the mechanism of diamond synthesis, and in 1966 a rare form of hexagonal diamond was named *lonsdaleite* in her honour. Her impish sense of humour was in evidence when she responded: "It makes me feel both proud and rather humble that it shall be called lonsdaleite. Certainly the name seems appropriate since the mineral only occurs in very small quantities (perhaps rare would be too flattering) and it is generally rather mixed up!"[8] When she took up the study of kidney- and other stones in the 1960s, she loved to show an X-ray photo of Napoleon III's bladder stone.[9]

From 1943 to the end of her life Kathleen travelled the world lecturing and visiting scientific colleagues. Fittingly, her first trip abroad was to Ireland, in 1943, when she returned home to visit the Dublin Institute for Advanced Studies (DIAS) to lecture at a summer school, chaired by Nobel physicist and DIAS professor, Erwin Schrödinger, and attended by the then Taoiseach, Éamon de Valera. She also made time to travel to Newbridge, her birthplace. Lonsdale visited many countries after the war including Russia and China, and as a result had trouble getting a visa to visit the USA. One embassy official told her: "You've been to the three most difficult places: Russia, China and gaol."

She was active in movements to promote peace, including the Pugwash Movement,[10] the Atomic Scientists' Association (of which she was a vice-president), and the Women's International League for Peace and Freedom (president). Often invited to speak at home and abroad, on topics such as science and religion, and the role of women in science, she advocated women's greater participation in science, and knew at first-hand the difficulties of combining marriage and a family with a professional career. Hodgkin quotes her as saying: "My own research life has been greatly enriched by having been broken into by periods of enforced change. I was not idle while I had my three children; far from it. But it gave me the opportunity of standing back, as it were, and looking at my work. And I came back with new ideas."

'Countries that want married women to return to science must make special arrangements to encourage them'

As for those women who made it through the glass ceiling, she knew that, even then, it was still a difficult balancing act: "Sir Lawrence Bragg once described the life of a university professor as similar to that of a queen bee, nurtured, tended and cared for because she has only one function in life. Nothing could be farther from the life of the average professional woman."[11] These reservations aside, she had strong views on the need to encourage and support women who wanted to have a family and use their scientific talents and, in 1970, the year before her death, said that any country that wants to make full use of all its potential scientists and technologists could do so, but it must not expect to get the women quite so simply as it gets the men. "Is it Utopian, then, to suggest that any country that really wants married women to return to a scientific career, when her children no longer need her physical presence, should make special arrangements to encourage her to do so?"[12]

She helped start the Young Scientist's section of the British Association for the Advancement of Science (BAAS), making a note to herself: "Never refuse an opportunity to speak in schools." Her commitment and dedication to the cause may well have paid off: a survey of crystallographers in the early 1990s showed that 14% were women, compared to just 2% of all physicists. This is probably due first, to the influences of William and Lawrence Bragg, and later J.D. Bernal, all of whom encouraged women in their discipline, and then to the influence of Kathleen Lonsdale herself, who was one of the most famous women in British science from the 1930s to 1971.

The 1943 summer school organised in Dublin by Nobel physicist, Erwin Schrödinger includ-ed a reception at the President of Ireland's residence, Áras an Uachtaráin, in the Phoenix Park. Prof Schrödinger (left to right), Prof Max Born, Dr Kathleen Lonsdale, An Uachtarán (President) Dr Douglas Hyde, Prof P.P. Ewald, and An Taoiseach, Éamon de Valera. Image: courtesy, The Irish Times

In 1965, when Thomas retired, the Lonsdales moved to Bexhill-on-Sea, which meant five hours commuting each day to work. Kathleen retired three years later, in 1968, and was honoured by being made an emeritus professor at UCL, which allowed her to continue working and publishing to the end of her life. In the year of her retirement, she was elected the first woman president of the BAAS and the title she chose for her presidential address was 'Science and the Good Life'. Her sense of humour shone through when she explained she had chosen the title "even though some of you, knowing that I am a vegetarian and a teetotaller, may wonder what I know about the good life anyhow." But, she explained that she had loved her work and was, even then, after 45 years of scientific research, excited and thrilled by new facts about crystals and their properties:

"Non-scientists sometimes wonder what aesthetic pleasure there can be in making patterns or equations by means of mathematical calculation or in the use of scientific equipment, such as an X-ray diffraction camera, an electron microscope, or an ordinary or polarising microscope? But no-one who has seen illustrations of magnified snowflakes, the optic colours of a thin crystal or the diffraction patterns of, say, a diamond plate taken with a divergent X-ray beam can doubt that these things are lovely in the themselves." [13]

Unfortunately, Lonsdale became ill with cancer soon afterwards. In December 1970, she was admitted to hospital, but carried on working from her sick-bed. Shortly after celebrating Thomas's 70th birthday, she died, on April 1st 1971, aged 68. A decade later, the chemistry building at University College, London was renamed the Kathleen Lonsdale Building in her honour. In 1998, the new Aeronautical and Environmental Building at the University of Limerick was officially named the Kathleen Lonsdale Building, marking her Irish birth. NUI Maynooth instituted a Lonsdale scholarship to mark her connection with Kildare, and a commemorative plaque was erected at the former Yardley family home in Newbridge, Co Kildare, in 2003. Kathleen Lonsdale's achievements are lauded in the words of J.M. Robertson, in the *Dictionary of Scientific Biography*: "Kathleen Lonsdale had a profound influence on the development of X-ray crystallography and related fields in chemistry and physics. Very few have made so many important advances in so many different directions." [14]

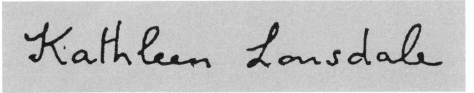

Signature: courtesy, the Royal Society

Associated places
Charlotte House, Charlotte Street, Newbridge County Kildare – former family home.
Kathleen Lonsdale Building, University of Limerick.

ENIAC, the world's first electronic computer, was a veritable behemoth, as evidenced in this publicity image circa 1946. With no manual, the women programmers had to have an engineer's understanding of the machine. Image: courtesy the Computer History Museum, California

One of the World's First Computer Programmers

Donegal-born mathematician, Kathleen 'Kay' McNulty Mauchly Antonelli (1921-2006), was one of the six ENIAC women who learned how to program the first digital computer, built for the US military during World War II. With no manual, they had to understand how the machine was built and worked, and together they helped to inaugurate the field of modern computing.

by Karlin Lillington

The first 'computer' was not a machine – it was a woman. The term was the formal job title given to women in the 1890s who manually computed complex astronomical calculations,[1] and later to the dozens of women employed by the USA military during the Second World War to manually calculate the flight path of a bullet or shell from the moment it left the muzzle of a gun until it landed. Among the latter was a young Irish-born woman, Kathleen 'Kay' McNulty, who would go on to become one of the world's first digital computer programmers.

Kay McNulty was born on February 12th, 1921 in the Creeslough area of Co Donegal. Her father James was a stone mason and active in the struggle for Irish independence from Britain. A member of the Irish Republican Army and a commandant of the Doe Battalion of the Irish Volunteers, he was arrested on the

'I just knew I loved math': Kay McNulty on her high-school graduation, 1938. Image: Wikimedia Commons

night of Kay's birth and imprisoned for two years. After his release, and when Kay was three, James McNulty took his wife, Anne Nellis McNulty, and six children to the United States, and established a masonry business in Philadelphia, Pennsylvania. Kay grew up in the Wyndmoor and historic Chestnut Hill suburbs of Philadelphia. According to her children, she spoke only Irish at home until she was sent to primary school. She later attended Hallahan Catholic High School in Philadelphia. At school, Kay excelled at mathematics and went on to take a degree in the subject at Chestnut Hill College for Women, a small Catholic college, in 1942. Her coursework included classes in algebra, history of mathematics, integral calculus, spherical trigonometry, differential calculus, and partial differential equations. Few women at the time took science and technology degrees – only three in her class of 92 graduated in mathematics. "In those days not many women majored in math," she said. "I always had an interest in statistics, and I thought, well, I might work in an insurance company or something. I just didn't know. I just knew I loved math; that was the only thing I was really good at. It was one of those subjects you don't have to study. No matter what the problem is, you just sit down and work it out like a puzzle."

When Kay reached the third year of her four-year degree course, she was already thinking about how she would find work with her unusual mathematics qualification. She was not interested in teaching, and insurance companies required a Masters degree for actuarial positions – she also found out later that they seldom hired women. "The best bet was some business training for me. So I took as many business courses as I could squeeze in: accounting, money and banking, business law, economics and statistics." Normally, women would have had a hard time finding mathematics-related jobs, but Kay graduated in the middle of wartime America. With the USA facing a severe shortage of the men who would normally be employed in the area, she found she now had skills that were in great demand.

Soon after graduation, she came across an advertisement placed in a Philadelphia newspaper which stated: "The need for women engineers and scientists is growing both in industry and government. Women are being offered scientific and engineering jobs where formerly men were preferred. Now is the time to consider your job in science and engineering . . . you will find that the slogan there as elsewhere is 'Women Wanted!'" She and her friend Fran Bilas responded to the ad – which Kay said reminded her of a 'Wanted' poster for Wild West outlaws – and were told the US Army's Ballistics Research Laboratory in Maryland was looking for women to work in its division at the Moore School of Electrical Engineering at the University of Pennsylvania.

The work entailed calculating trajectories for shells and bullets, crucial information for soldiers using big artillery guns. The Army issued printed tables that enabled soldiers to know how to position the muzzle of a gun depending on the distance and position of the target and taking account of a wide range of additional factors such as wind speed. Hand computing the trajectories was dull, intensive work using paper and pencil and a desktop mechanical calculator. A single trajectory took 30 to 40 hours to solve – a full week's work – and each table contained some 2,000 to 4,000 trajectories. The women accepted the job, with the formal title 'computer, SP-4', a sub-professional ('SP') civil service-grade job considered the equivalent of clerical work. Men employed in similar work were categorised as professional mathematicians, and were paid more, according to Kay. "The pay was not spectacular (less than $2,000 annually), but at that time, and with no work experience, it was very welcome," said Kay.

Neither Kay nor her friend Fran knew anything about calculating trajectories because the process involved numerical integration, an area of mathematics that was not on the curriculum at Chestnut Hill. They confessed their lack of knowledge and, according to Kay, were handed a thick book on numerical integration and left to figure it out for themselves. "Fran and I read the book, and we still didn't know what to do," Kay recalled many years later. "It was so complicated. . . It is a very complex equation; it has about 15 multiplications and a square root and I don't know what else. You have to find out where the bullet is every 10th of a second from the time it leaves the muzzle of the gun, and you have to take into account all the things that are going to affect the path of the bullet." Eventually someone handed them sheets of paper and walked them through the equations step by step. At that point, said Kay, they understood the arithmetic involved, figured out what was expected, and got to work. The women were worked in exhausting 48-hour shifts, with Kay eventually becoming a shift leader.

Several weeks after they started working at the Moore School, they were given the chance to run the equations on a prized calculating machine belonging to the school and called the differential analyzer. This huge machine had an electric motor but was still an analogue calculator, and the arithmetic was performed by rotating gears and shafts. Yet, it could calculate a single trajectory in 45 minutes, compared to the five days it took the women to do just one by hand. However, with up to 4,000 trajectories in each table, even the differential analyzer needed a month to compute one table.

The war effort clearly needed faster calculations, and the Moore School was coming under pressure from the Army's top brass to provide them. J. Presper Eckert, an engineer at the school, had already been brought in to figure out ways of hastening the calculating process on the differential analyzer. He quickly realised that analogue machines, with their mechanical limitations, simply could not be pushed much further. He was convinced that an electronic calculating machine – an electronic, rather than a human, computer – was the answer. His colleague and friend John Mauchly, another Moore School engineer with a special bent for electronics, agreed, and the problem captured the two men's attention and imagination. Over many months, through trial and error, they slowly worked out the basic idea for the world's first general purpose digital computer, called ENIAC (Electronic Numerical Integrator and Computer). More importantly, Eckert and Mauchly eventually received the go-ahead to assemble a team and secretly build it.

The resulting mammoth machine had 40 eight-foot high black panelled modules, 18,000 vacuum tubes and 3,000 switches, but no memory to hold instructions on how it was to perform a calculation. Instead, it had to be programmed by hand, in a process reminiscent of an operator working on a giant telephone

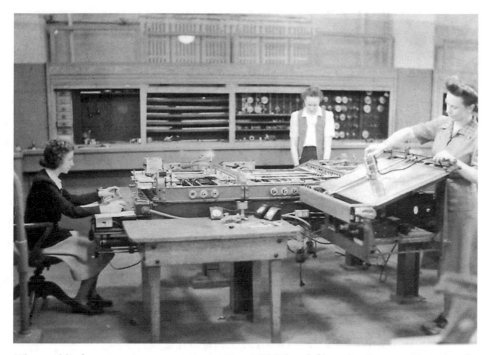

The world's first computer programmers: Kay McNulty (left), and colleagues Alyse Snyder and Sis Stump with the differential analyzer, in the basement of the Moore School of Electrical Engineering, University of Pennsylvania, circa 1942-1945. The analyzer was an analogue calculator, used to compute trajectories before the creation of the ENIAC electronic computer. Image: Wikimedia Commons

switchboard: cables were plugged in here, unplugged there, and dials and switches were set by hand for every single calculation. Punch cards could also be used to submit data to the giant (see Panel). Because ENIAC was to be used to calculate trajectories, Kay and five of the other best women 'computers' at Moore School – Jean Jennings Bartik, Frances 'Betty' Snyder Holberton, Marlyn Wescoff Meltzer, Frances Bilas Spence and Ruth Lichterman Teitelbaum – were transferred to work on ENIAC. Their job would be to programme ENIAC to perform the calculations. But this was a serious challenge.

"There were no manuals," said Kay. "They gave us all the blueprints, and we could ask the engineers anything. We had to learn how the machine was built, what each tube did. We had to study how the machine worked and figure out how to do a job on it. So we went right ahead and taught ourselves how to program." This involved figuring out how to break down the complex trajectory

How to program a behemoth

THE ENIAC is considered to be the first functional ancestor of today's desktop computer. But comparing ENIAC to a PC is a bit like noting the relationship between a brontosaurus and a sparrow. They are related, but looking at them side by side, you would be hard pressed to see how. First off, the ENIAC was, literally, a giant. Weighing close to 30 tons, it was the size of a railway car and filled most of the room. ENIAC had 40 modular memory and processing units, each in its own 3 metre-high cabinet. Plus 3,000 switches and 18,000 vacuum tubes, generating so much heat that it needed industrial fans to cool the components and keep them from melting.

If ENIAC made an obvious processing error, it was the job of Kay McNulty and the other ENIAC women to track down the single broken vacuum tube responsible for the error, among the 18,000 tubes in the machine. Initially, a tube or two malfunctioned every day. Programming the behemoth often took up to two days. Because software (which conveys instructions directly to a computer), had not yet been invented, and ENIAC did not have a hard drive to store instructions (another invention that was still several years away), the program commands all had to be entered by hand into ENIAC.

This was done by the women, who carried detailed instruction diagrams and equations into smaller units that ENIAC could manage, then integrate all the smaller results back into the correct answer. They then proceeded to programme a trajectory to go on to the machine. "We had barely begun to think that we had enough knowledge of the machine to programme a trajectory, when we were told that two people were coming from Los Alamos [the New Mexico laboratory for the USA's secret Manhattan Project to develop an atomic bomb] to put a problem on the machine."

Though there was much background concern that ENIAC might not work, the women programmed this new problem into the machine and, weeks later, learned that the calculation had been successful, proving the ENIAC's ability to walked along the huge banks of processing units, plugging and unplugging cables and setting dials. Punch cards, made by IBM, were also used to enter data. The thousands of cards needed to perform calculations were fed into punch card readers adapted for ENIAC. Again, this was considered a woman's job. Pictures of ENIAC from the 1940s and '50s show immaculately-dressed women in skirts, busily adjusting dials on the machine or poised to feed stacks of punch cards into its readers.

ENIAC's first big job, also used to test its accuracy, was a secret calculation relating to the trigger for the hydrogen bomb, being developed during World War II under strict security at the Los Alamos nuclear laboratory. Kay, who noted afterwards that she was not sure Eckert and Mauchly were ever told the nature of the Los Alamos problem, was among the handful of trusted women programmers who were set the task of preparing the machine's plugs and switches to work out the calculations.

One million punch cards were needed for the complex problem. Because ENIAC's memory was so limited, the problem had to be completed in stages, with intermediate results printed out and new punch cards prepared. Just under a month later, the result came in, and the calculation proved that ENIAC worked. The director of Los Alamos sent a pleased note to the Moore School: "It is clear that physics as well as other sciences will profit greatly from the development of such machines."

handle the most complicated mathematical problems. ENIAC was immediately put to work computing trajectories, performing the calculations in 15 seconds. "ENIAC made me . . . obsolete," Kay later reminisced. At first, due to the secrecy of the project, the women were not even allowed to see ENIAC: they had to figure out how to set the switches and plugs for each equation from studying the blueprints, then submit the settings in the form of charts to the men, who would carry them out. Eventually, the women obtained the security clearance to enable them to work directly on ENIAC themselves.

A few months after the secret Manhattan Project calculation was successfully completed, the US Government decided ENIAC could be unveiled to the world. On Valentine's Day, 1946, a formal event was held that received wide coverage in the national press. ENIAC was set a number of calculations that the *New York Times* said "took place in less than the wink of an eye" – failing to recognise the many hours it took the women programmers to set up the calculation. The newspaper was impressed: "Leaders who saw the device in action for the first time heralded it as a tool with which to begin to rebuild scientific affairs on new foundations." At the event, the men involved with ENIAC's development lined up for photographs while the women 'computers' stood in the background and their role as programmers was not acknowledged at all. Kay later quipped that she feared they were viewed as decorative "refrigerator women" – advertising models demonstrating a new appliance – and attendees "thought we were just window dressing," she said. One amusing footnote to the press event is that ENIAC's engineers, worried that the audience would not be sufficiently impressed by a machine that did not seem to be doing anything at all while it calculated, rigged up a panel of light bulbs on which they painted numbers. Certain bulbs would light up as the calculation was performed, making for a modestly flashy but generally meaningless show. Yet newsreel footage of the event profoundly influenced how computers would be represented in films and on television for decades: computers from *Star Trek* to *2001: A Space Odyssey* to *Star Wars* always have panels of flashing lights.

Kay McNulty continued to work on ENIAC for two more years until, in 1948, she married ENIAC co-inventor John Mauchly, whose first wife had died in a drowning accident. By this time Mauchly and Eckert were running their own computer company which produced one of the first commercial computers, the UNIVAC. Kay left work at this time to be a full-time housewife and to raise seven children. However, she continued to work with her husband on computer program designs and techniques. John Mauchly died in 1980, and five years later Kay married Severo Antonelli, a renowned photographer of the Italian Futurist School; Severo Antonelli died in 1996.

After John Mauchly's death, Kay began to argue publicly for his and Presper Eckert's recognition as the co-inventors of the first general purpose electronic computer, a matter that has remained the subject of much heated dispute amongst computing historians, and even the people who were at Moore School at the time. A major federal patent case in the 1970s failed to clarify the issue, with the judge's decision seeming to acknowledge the pair as the inventors but also giving that designation to a rival at Iowa State University, John Atanasoff. In 1984, Kay published a controversial article entitled 'John Mauchly's early years' in the influential professional journal *Annals of the History of Computing*, in which she carefully laid out evidence for their pioneering role and achievement.[2] So hotly contested was this subject, that the biographies editor for the journal wrote a foreword explaining why he felt it was important for someone with Kay's insights to publish such an article. He also noted that three of the journal's own referees for the paper disagreed with her conclusions and planned to publish rebuttals.

Around this time, Kay was increasingly in demand as a speaker on ENIAC, computing history, and the role that she and her women colleagues played in the development of modern computing. In 1997, she was inducted into the Women in Technology International (WITI) Hall of Fame. Her oral history was recorded in 1998, and is part of a documentary film about the ENIAC programmers called 'The Computers'. She was also honoured by Letterkenny Institute of Technology in her home county of Donegal, which established an annual award for the best computer science student each year, the Kay McNulty medal and prize.

Yet even well into the 1990s, Kay McNulty Mauchly Antonelli and the other ENIAC women were still considered afterthoughts in the history of the machine, and computing generally, though they were the world's first computer programmers, in the modern sense of the word. One, Betty Snyder Holberton, wrote the C-10 instruction code for UNIVAC, making programming much simpler, and went on to help develop COBOL and FORTRAN, two of the first computer languages, yet this was barely acknowledged for years. Even when Kay was invited to attend the 40th anniversary celebrations for ENIAC at the University of Pennsylvania in 1986, it was not to celebrate her own achievements but rather to speak, and be honoured, as John Mauchly's widow. None of the other women programmers was recognised at the event. Even by 1996, ENIAC's 50th anniversary, the University of Pennsylvania initially had no plans to recognise the ENIAC women.

The achievements of Kay and her five women colleagues only began to be truly appreciated – and marvelled at – by the computing establishment in that 50th anniversary year, as their pivotal programming role became clear when they were

The annual McNulty medal for the best computer science student at Letterkenny Institute of Technology. Image: © Letterkenny IT

interviewed for a number of articles. W. Barkley Fritz, who became an ENIAC programmer in 1948, interviewed several of the women in the mid-1990s and noted: "[L]earning to program ENIAC required a complete understanding of how the machine was designed. They learned how ENIAC worked by talking with the original design engineers, studying their logic diagrams, and sharing ideas with the other programmers. At the very beginning they were not even able to get hands-on experience on ENIAC. When they did get access to the machine, they began to understand something of the unreliability of the vacuum tube technology of the time, and they realized the necessity of learning how to trouble-shoot the machine as well as their program."

Another article published the same year described how complicated their job was: "The first task was breaking down complex differential equations into the smallest possible steps. Each of these had to be routed to the proper bank of electronics and performed in sequence – not simply a linear progression but a parallel one, for the ENIAC, amazingly, could conduct many operations simultaneously. Every datum and instruction had to reach the correct location in time for the operation that depended on it, to within 1/5000th of a second." In other words, the women were not just programmers in today's sense of the word, but had to acquire an engineer's understanding of how the computer worked, and how to fix it when problems arose. They also required a thorough understanding of the mathematics behind every problem submitted to ENIAC. The six women probably had a more complete and thorough understanding of ENIAC's construction and operation than many of the men who designed it.

Kathleen McNulty Mauchly Antonelli and the other ENIAC women did indeed push frontiers. Through their work, they significantly advanced the budding field of computing. Amongst them, they invented the field of modern computer programming and were the world's first computer programmers of general purpose electronic computers. In the absence of manuals, and needing to explain how to program ENIAC, they came up with techniques still used today: specific formats for flowcharts and programs; the use of logical block diagrams; techniques for debugging programs and hardware.

After a brief illness, Kathleen McNulty Mauchly Antonelli died of cancer in Wyndmoor, Pemnnsylvania, aged 85, on April 20th, 2006. Of her own pioneering involvement with the development of computing, Kay always remained modest and enthusiastic about the overall achievement: "There was always the sense we were pushing frontiers," she said. "It was F-U-N all the time."

Notes and Sources

Foreword, pp 1-7

Further reading

Creese, Mary R.S., *Ladies in the Laboratory? American and British Women in Science, 1800-1900* (Lanham: Scarecrow Press, 1998).

Gates, Barbara T., *Kindred Nature: Victorian and Edwardian Women Embrace the Living World* (Chicago University Press, 1998).

Gates, Barbara T., and Ann B. Shteir, eds. *Natural Eloquence: Women Reinscribe Science* (Madison: University of Wisconsin Press, 1997)

Sheffield, Suzanne L., *Revealing New Worlds: Three Victorian Women Naturalists* (London: Routledge, 2001).

1 The word "scientist" was coined by William Whewell in a speech in 1832; it was not generally used in British/Irish English until the 1880s, but was adopted more quickly in American English.

2 The insistence on formal qualification made it difficult for women to participate in other professions, too.

1. 'Laurels for fair as well as manly brows', pp 8-21

Barrett, W. F., *An historical sketch of the Royal College of Science from its foundation to the year 1900.* Falconer, Dublin (1907)

Bowler, Peter J. and Nicholas Whyte (eds), *Science and society in Ireland: the social context of science and technology in Ireland, 1800-1950.* QUB, Belfast (1997)

Clarke, D. 'An outline of the history of science in Ireland', *Studies*, lxii (1973), pp 287-302.

Clarke, D. 'Sir Robert Kane', *Administration*, 16 (1968), pp 155-59.

Clarke, D. 'The contribution of the Royal Dublin Society to science and technology in Ireland', *Administration*, 15, no. 1 (1967) pp 23-34.

College of Science Association, *College of Science for Ireland: its origin and development, with notes on similar institutions in other countries, and a bibliography of the work published by the staff and students 1900-1923*, Dublin (1923)

Crawford, Elizabeth, *The woman's suffrage movement in Britain and Ireland: a regional survey* Routledge, London (2006)

Daly, Mary E., *Dublin, the deposed capital: a social and economic history, 1860-1914* Cork University Press, Cork (1984)

Freeman's Journal, 29 May 1856 and 21 October 1859.

General descriptive guide to the Museum of Irish Industry, Dublin. Thom, Dublin (1857)

Jarrell, Richard A., 'The Department of Science and Art and control of Irish science, 1853-1905', *Irish Historical Studies*, xxiii, no. 92 (1983), pp 330-47.

Johnston, Roy, 'Science and technology in Irish national culture', *The Crane Bag*, vii, no. 2 (1983), pp 58-63.

Kane, Robert John, *The industrial resources of Ireland* (2nd ed.) Hodges, Dublin (1845)

Keating, Pat, 'Sir Robert Kane and the Museum of Irish Industry' in *Proceedings of the Conference of the Educational Studies Association of Ireland, 1980*, pp 276-86. Limerick (1980).

Kelham, Brian, 'The Royal College of Science for Ireland (1867-1926)', *Studies*, lvi (1967), pp 297-309.

Kerr, J.J. 'Sir Robert Kane: an apostle of Irish industries', *Dublin Historical Record*, v, no. 4, (1943), pp 137-46.

McMillan, Norman (ed.), *Prometheus's fire: a history of scientific and technological education in Ireland.* Tyndall Publications, Kilkenny (2002)

Meenan, James and D. Clarke (eds.), *RDS: the Royal Dublin Society, 1731-1981* Gill and Macmillan, Dublin (1981)

Mollan, Charles, William Davis and Brendan Finucane (eds) *Irish innovators in science and technology.* RIA, Dublin (2002)

O Raghallaigh, Deasmumhan, *Sir Robert Kane: a pioneer in science, industry & commerce, first president of Queen's College Cork.* Cork University Press, Cork (1942)

Owens, Rosemary Cullen, *A social history of women in Ireland, 1870-1970* Gill and Macmillan, Dublin (2005)

Raftery, Deirdre and Susan M. Parkes, *Female education in Ireland, 1700–1900: Minerva or Madonna,* Irish Academic Press, (Dublin (2007)

1   Mulvihill, Mary, ed. *Stars, Shells and Bluebells,* WITS, Dublin (1997)

2   McKenna-Lawlor, Susan, *Whatever shines should be observed,* Kluwer, Dublin (1998)

3   Stewart, A.T.Q. *Belfast Royal Academy: the first century, 1785-1885* (Antrim, 1985); quoted by Helena C.G. Chesney, 'Enlightenment and education', in J.W. Foster and H.C.G. Chesney, (eds.), *Nature in Ireland: a scientific and cultural history,* Lilliput, Dublin, (1997), p.380.

4   *Reports from the Select Committees on Foundation Schools and Education in Ireland; together with the Minutes of Evidence, Appendix and Index.* [Wyse] Part I: 1835, Part II: 1836, p. 327, H.C. 1835 (630).

5   Wheeler, T.S. 'Sir Robert Kane – life and work', *Studies*, xxxiii (June and Sept 1944), pp 185-68, 286-88.

6   *Freeman's Journal*, 21 Oct. 1859.

7   *Programme of educational arrangements for the session of 1860-61*, [Museum of Irish Industry]. Thom, Dublin, 1860, p. 7.

8   *Third Report of the Department of Science and Art*, p. 131, H.C. 1856 [2123] xxiv, 1.

9   *Freeman's Journal*, 21 Oct. 1859.

10 *Daily Express*, 15 June 1858.

11 *Freeman's Journal*, 29 May 1856.

12 *Dublin Builder*, 1 Nov. 1859; *Freeman's Journal*, 21 Oct. 1859.

13 *Report from the Commission on the Science and Art Department in Ireland*; Vol. 1 Report, *p. xxxiii*, H.C. 1868-9 [4103], xxiv,1.

14 UCD Archives, Royal College of Science for Ireland, minutes of meeting, 28 Nov. 1867 (UCDA, RCSI/1).

15 Barrett, W.F., *An historical sketch of the Royal College of Science from its foundation to the year 1900*, Falconer, Dublin, 1907, p. 9.

16 O'Connor Aine V. and Susan Parkes, *Gladly learn and gladly teach: Alexandra College and School, 1866-1966*, Blackwater Press, Dublin, 1966, p. 4.

17 E. Clibborn to Alexander Carte, 2 Oct. 1865 (Natural History Museum Dublin, correspondence files, C file).

18 Kate to Alexander Leeper, 6, 12 July 1921; Cecilia to Alexander Leeper, 27 July 1921; quoted by John Poynter, *Doubts and uncertainties: a life of Alexander Leeper*, Melbourne University Press, Melbourne, 1997, p. 399.

19 David Moore acknowledged him in his *Cybele Hibernica*; David Moore and Alexander Goodman More, *Contributions towards a Cybele Hibernica, being outlines of the geographical distribution of plants in Ireland*, Hodges, Dublin, 1866, p. v.

20 *The Irish flora; comprising the Phaenogamous [flowering] plants and ferns*, Hodges and Smith, Dublin 1846 [re-issue of 1833 edition], p. ix.

21 David Moore and Alexander Goodman More, *op. cit.*, p. vii.

22 Praeger, R.L. *Some Irish naturalists: a biographical notebook,* Dundalk, Tempest Press, (1948) p.111.

23 Wheeler, T.S., 'Sir Robert Kane: life and work' in *Studies*, xxxiii (1944), pp 165-6; John P. Cullinane, 'Katherine Sophia Baily (Lady Kane): botanist and wife of Sir Robert Kane, first President of Queen's College, Cork' in *U.C.C. Record*, No 46 (1971), p.20.

24 Bailey, S. [Katherine Sophia], 'On planting foreign pines' in *Irish Farmer's and Gardener's Magazine*, i (1834), pp 262-9; Bailey, S, 'Observations on some foreign trees suited to Ireland' in *Irish Farmer's and Gardener's Magazine*, i (1834), pp 591-603.

25 *Transactions of the Botanical Society of Edinburgh* (1836), p. 49.

26 Cullinane, John P. *op.cit.* p.20.

27 Ferguson [Mary Catherine Guinness], Lady, in *Sir Samuel Ferguson in the Ireland of his day*. Vol. II, Blackwood, Edinburgh (1896), p. 178.

28 *Express*, 22 May 1873.

29 Murphy, John A. *The College: a history of Queen's/University College Cork, 1845–1995* Cork University press, Cork 1995, p. 74.

2. 'The Glorious Privilege', pp 22-35

For a full account of the Queens Institute, see: Phillips, Patricia. 'The Queen's Institute, Dublin (1861-1881): The First Technical College for Women in the British Isles', in: *Prometheus's Fire: A History of Scientific and Technological Education in Ireland*, ed. Dr. N. McMillan (Carlow, 2000) 446-463. Anon, Letter to the Archbishop of Dublin, undated (late 1880s?), Alexandra College Archive. Ergane, 'The Queen's Institute, For the Training and Employment of Educated Women', *Victoria*

Magazine, 1864, 457–466.

Jellicoe, Anne, 'The Condition of Young women employed in Manufactories in Dublin', *Transactions of the National Association for the Promotion of Social Science*, 1861, 640–645.

Jellicoe, Anne, 'A Visit to the Female Convict Prison at Mountjoy, Dublin', *Transactions of the National Association for the Promotion of Social Science*, 1862, 437–442.

The Quakers of Mountmellick. A Short History of the Religious Society of Friends in the Town of Mountmellick 1650–1900, produced by a FÁS training unit and sponsored by Mountmellick Development Association (1994).

1   The first Quaker Meeting in Ireland was set up in 1654 by William Edmundson who was involved in the Ulster linen industry. Later, a sizeable group moved to Cavan to avoid the persecution to which their radical ideas and conflict with the Established Church exposed them. A settlement was then established at Mountmellick and Rosenallis.

2   William Edmundson came to Ireland because his brother suggested that there were "presentations and opportunities to get riches" either by trading or taking land. *Friends Historical Tour. Irish Midland Counties*, September 2000, p.13

3   During this industrial heyday *c.* 4,000 were employed in Quaker industries in Mountmellick. The town was an important centre for Friends in Ireland for *c.* 200 years although by 1876 numbers had dwindled to 109 members spread over six meetings. The town had an industrial base with iron, woollen and cotton manufacture, which had taken over earlier enterprises of brewing and malting. A branch of the Grand Canal reached the town in the 1830s. Ibid., p.10.

4   *The Parochial School Returns* (1835) noted 10 schools deemed "Protestant", although many were in fact Quaker, and a well–attended Sunday School. Several of these schools catered for the better–off, e.g. the Leinster Provincial School, a Quaker establishment, where fees were £24 per annum and the school house had been built by the Society of Friends at a cost of £1800. At Anne Shannon's school for girls, which opened *c.* 1790s (at the time of the inspection she had been sole proprietor for 37 years) the fees were 28 guineas per annum. On the other hand, Eliza Murphy's school cost about tuppence halfpenny a week.

5   ibid, pp. 298–299

6   See Jane Houston–Almqvist, *Mountmellick Work* (Dublin, 1985), passim. Mrs Carter used readily available materials, cotton on cotton, all in white. Her designs were bold, and her work was much admired and sought after.

7   Anne and John Jellicoe (1819–1862) were married in 1846. A "miller of Monasterevan", he was the son of John and Elizabeth Jellicoe of Flemingston, Tipperary, had been a pupil at Newtown School Waterford 1830–33, and came to Monasterevan in 1845. Milling was another Quaker enterprise. The young couple lived in Mountmellick until 1846 when they moved to nearby Clara in King's County (now Co Offaly). He acquired a flour mill there which burnt down but, soon afterwards, was rebuilt. They were friends with the Goodbody family, a prominent local Quaker family.

8   See Almqvist, op.cit, p. 12

9   Isabella Mulvaney, Obituary, *Englishwoman's Review*, November 15th, 1880, p.518

10   Unpublished diary of Lydia Goodbody, *Portfolio 21* of Hugh Goodbody Collection, Society of Friends, Dublin. Entry for 20 February 1854.

11   The Dublin Statistical Society survives as the Statistical and Social Inquiry Society of Ireland.

12   S. Shannon Millin, *Our Society: Its Aims and Achievements 1847–1919*, read on 9th January 1919.

13   Ibid, p.613

14   Chief among these were William Neilson Hancock (1820-88), John Kells Ingram (1823-1907) and Richard Chenevix Trench (1807-86)

15   *Transactions of the National Association for the Promotion of Social Science* (London) 1861, p. 641

16   The jobs open to working-class women could be divided into skilled and unskilled. The first group tended to protect their craft from newcomers. These trades included "the winding of silk, the weaving of carriage lace; hat, cap and bonnet making, tailoring, bootclosing, brush and pin–making, bookbinding etc" [Transactions 1861, p.640] Unskilled jobs included weaving linen, cotton, frieze, making up clothing and the paper trade in most of its branches. The average wage was about six shilllings a week. Men, on the other hand, could earn more than four times that "but cannot be induced to make provision for a 'rainy day'." Bookbinding was one trade that could offer a woman a better deal: Anne Jellicoe noted that in one house a woman was successfully managing a machine previously worked by a man. The average wage was better and, significantly, "[t]hough not required to read or write while occupied in the lower departments, education greatly facilitates their rise in the trade" (p.641).

17   Ibid p.645

18   *Transactions of the National Association for the Promotion of Social Science Glasgow 1860* (1861), p.xviii–xx. See also, Patricia Phillips, 'The Queen's Institute, Dublin (1861-1881): The First Technical College for Women in the British Isles', in: *Prometheus's Fire: A History of Scientific and Technological Education in Ireland*, ed. Dr. N. McMillan, Carlow (2000) 447-454.

19   See the portrayals of the governess in 19th-century novels, e.g. Anthony Trollope and, Mrs Gaskill. Charlotte Bronte's Jane Eyre was the exception!

20   S. Shannon Millin, op cit p.615

21   'Twenty Years' History of the Queen's Institute and College Dublin', *Journal of the Women's Education Union* (London, 1881) p.170

22   'The Queen's Institute, For the Training and Employment of Educated Women. An Industrial college for Women in Dublin', *Victoria Magazine* (London, 1864) p460

23   "…that moral panic which is often fatally powerful to prevent new suggestions from undergoing experimental tests, and a certificate of prosperity proves truly conservative", Ibid. p.457

24   Ibid, p. 459

25   Ibid, p. 460

26   See, Patricia Phillips, *op.cit. passim*

27   *Victoria Magazine, op.cit.* p.462.

28   Anne was John's sole heir. In his will (9 July 1850) he referred to his wife as "my beloved Annie".

29   Obituary in *The Englishwoman's Review*, November 13th, 1880, p.516

30   Anne Jellicoe, 'Alexandra College, Dublin', *Journal of the Women's Education* (1873), p.55-56. See also: *Return from Alexandra College to the Powis Commission, Vol. VIII. Miscellaneous Papers*, 1870 (C.6VII) XXVIII, part v, p. 916

31   A.B Corlett, 'Twenty Years' History of the Queen's Institute and College, Dublin', *Journal of the Women's Education Union* (1881), 170-172

32   See, Patricia Phillips, *op.cit. passim*

33   The death certificate, issued at West Bromwich, details "Cancer of the Uterus" and "Phlebitis"

as the causes of death

34 Unpublished letter in the archives of Alexandra College

35 See, for example, Judith Harford, 'The movement for the higher education of women in Ireland: gender equality or denominational rivalry', *History of Education* September, 2005, vol. 34, no. 5, p. 502

36 *Journal of the Women's Education Union* (November 15, 1880), p. 171

3. First in their Field, pp 36-47

1 Ford, Connie M. *Aleen Cust Veterinary Surgeon – Britain's First Woman Vet*, Biopress, Bristol (1990)

2 Beggs, R. 'Lilian Bland: Pioneer Extraordinary' in: *Ulster Folk & Transport Museum Year Book* 1977/78

3 Letter from Lilian Bland to *Flight*, February 1910

4 Byrne, Liam *History of Aviation in Ireland,* Blackwater Press, Dublin (1980)

5 *Belfast News Letter*, August 13th 2004

6 Geraghty, Sidney. 'The First Woman Engineer?', *Engineers Journal* March/April (1998) p31-33

7 *Connaught Champion*, Feb 23, 1907

8 *Irish Law Reports*, 1940 [IR.] 316

9 Murphy-Lawless, J. and McCarthy, J. 'Social Policy and Fertility Change in Ireland: The Push to Legislate in Favour of Women's Agency', *European Journal of Women's Studies* 6 (1999) pp69-96,

10 Drew, E. 'Part-Time Working in Ireland: Meeting the Flexibility Needs of Women Workers or Employers?', *Canadian Journal of Irish Studies* 18, 1 (1992) p95-P109.

11 Central Statistics Office

4. Erratics, Intrusions and Graptolites, pp 48-59

Bibliography

Sydney Mary Thompson (Madame Christen):

'A plea for Irish glaciology', *Irish Naturalist* 3 (1894), 30-34.

'The common mussel (*Mytilus edulis*)', *Irish Naturalist* 3 (1894), 176.

'The Belfast Field Club in Donegal', *Irish Naturalist* 3 (1894), 225-230.

'Irish Field Club Union. Report of the conference and excursion held at Galway on July 11th to 17th 1895. II. Geology', *Irish Naturalist* 4 (1895), 235-237.

'Feathered pensioners', *Irish Naturalist* 5 (1896), 118-119.

'Glacial geology of Kerry', *Irish Naturalist* 8 (1899), 61.

'The supposed occurrence of White Lias at Macedon Pt.', *Irish Naturalist* 9 (1900), 154.

'Report of the Geological Committee [1893-96]', *Proceedings of the Belfast Naturalists' Field Club* 4 (1901), 115-125, 229-231, 234-235, 302-310, 386-390.

'On the supposed occurrence of a patch of white Lias or Rhaetic rock on the shore N. of Macedon Point, Belfast Lough', *Proceedings of the Belfast Naturalists' Field Club* 4 (1901), 566-569.

'Investigations into the glacial drifts of the north-east of Ireland, conducted by the Naturalists' Field Club', *Irish Naturalist* **11** (1902), 275-276 [Madame Christen]

'A summary of the [B.N.F.] Club's recent glacial work', *Irish Naturalist* **15** (1906), 80 [Madame Christen] *Rodolphe Christen: the story of an artist's life, 1859-1906*. Longmans, Green & Co, London (1910).

Mary K. Andrews:

'Denudation at Cultra, Co. Down', *Proceedings of the Belfast Naturalists' Field Club* **3** (1893), 529-532; *Irish Naturalist* **2** (1893), 16-18, 47-49.

'Dykes in Antrim and Down', *Irish Naturalist* **3** (1894), 93-96.

'Erosion at Newcastle, Co. Down', *Irish Naturalist* **10** (1901), 114.

'Notes on Moel Tryfaen', *Proceedings of the Belfast Naturalists' Field Club* **4** (1901), 205-210.

Doris Reynolds (selected publications on Irish geology):

'The petrography of the Triassic sandstone of north-east Ireland', *Geological Magazine* **65** (1928), 448-473.

'The dykes of the Ards Peninsula', *Geological Magazine* **68** (1931), 97-111.

'The eastern end of the Newry Ingneous Complex', *Quarterly Journal of the Geological Society of London* **90** (1934), 585-636.

'Contact phenomena indicating a Tertiary age for the Gabbros of the Slieve Gullion District', *Proceedings of the Geologists' Association* **48** (1937), 247-275.

'The two monzonitic series of the Newry Complex', *Geological Magazine* **73** (1937), 337-364.

'The Albite-Schists of Antrim and their petrogenetic relationship to Caledonian orogenesis', *Proceedings of the Royal Irish Academy* **48B** (1942), 43-66.

'Granitization of hornfelsed diorite in the Newry granodiorite of Goraghwood Quarry, Co. Armagh', *Proceedings of the Royal Irish Academy* **48B** (1943), 231-267.

'The south-western end of the Newry Igneous Complex. A contribution towards the petrogenesis of the granodiorites', *Quarterly Journal of the Geological Society of London* **99** (1943), 205-246.

'The sequence of geochemical changes leading to granitisation', *Quarterly Journal of the Geological Society of London* **102** (1946), 390-447.

'The geology of Slieve Gullion, Foughill, and Carrickcarnon; an actualistic interpretation of a Tertiary gabbro-granophyre complex', *Transactions of the Royal Society of Edinburgh* **62** (1951), 85-142.

'Fluidization as a geologic process, and its bearing on the problem of intrusive granites', *American Journal of Science* **252** (1954), 577-614.

Veronica Conroy Burns:

Rickards, R.B., Burns, V. & Archer J.B. 'The Silurian sequence at Balbriggan, Co. Dublin', *Proceedings of the Royal Irish Academy* **73B** (1973), 303-316.

Burns, V. & Rickards, R.B. 'Silurian graptolite faunas of the Balbriggan Inlier, counties Dublin and Meath, and their evolutionary, stratigraphical and structural significance', *Proceedings of the Yorkshire Geological Society* **49** (1993), 283-291.

1   Higgs, B. and Wyse Jackson, P.N. 'The contribution of women to geological studies and education in Ireland', in: *The role of women in the history of geology*, edited by C.V. Burek and B. Higgs,

137-153. Geological Society, London, Special Publications **281** (2007).

2 Howarth, O.R.J. *The British Association for the Advancement of Science: a retrospect 1831–1931*. British Association for the Advancement of Science, London (1931).

3 A comprehensive account of the lives and work of these two ladies is given by M.R.S. and T.M. Creese in *Ladies in the Laboratory II: West European Women in Science, 1800-1900*. Scarecrow Press, Lanham, Maryland (2004), pp. 49-51.

4 Newmann, K. *Dictionary of Ulster Biography*. Institute of Irish Studies, Queen's University of Belfast, Belfast (1993).

5 *The Times*, Tuesday 11th September 1906.

6 Davis, W.J. 'Thomas Andrews', *Irish Innovators in Science and Technology*, edited by R.C. Mollan, W.J. Davis and B. Finucane, pp.114-115. Royal Irish Academy, Dublin (2002).

7 A list of the papers presented in the woman's convention is given in *American Naturalist* 1893, p. 1028.

8 Bancroft, H.H. *The Book of the Fair*. The Bancroft Company, Chicago and San Francisco (1893), p. 947.

9 Wyse Jackson, P.N. and Spencer Jones, M.E. 'The quiet workforce: the various roles of women in geological and natural history museums during the early to mid-1900s', *The role of women in the history of geology*, edited by C.V. Burek and B. Higgs, 97-113. Geological Society, London, Special Publications **281** (2007).

10 A sample of this unusual metamorphosed chalk can be found in the panelled entrance to the Office of Public Works at 51 St Stephen's Green, Dublin (see Wyse Jackson, P.N. *The Building Stones of Dublin: a walking guide*. Country House, Dublin (1993).

11 Gough, G.C. 'A case of metamorphism of Chalk', *Geological Magazine* **4** (1907), 145-148.

12 McHenry, A. 'Long excursion to Belfast, the coast of Antrim, and the Mourne Mountains', *Proceedings of the Geologists' Association* **14** (1896), 202.

13 Creese and Creese, *op. cit.* (2004), p. 51.

14 Wyse Jackson, P.N. 'Irish Rock Stars: Sydney Mary Thompson (Madame Christen) (1847-1923)', *Earth Science Ireland* **3** (2008), 14.

15 This was reprinted from the original BAAS Report as Wright, J. in Greenly, E. 'Report on the drift at Moel Tryfaen', *Geological Magazine* **47** (1900), 122-123.

16 Evans, E.E. and Turner, B.S. *Ireland's Eye: the photographs of Robert John Welch*. Blackstaff Press, Belfast (1977)

17 Wyse Jackson, P.N., 'On Rocks and Bicycles: a biobibliography of Grenville Arthur James Cole (1859-1924) fifth Director of the Geological Survey of Ireland', *Geological Survey of Ireland Bulletin* **4** (1989), 151-163.

18 Unpublished listing of Irish photographs in the BAAS Collection, Ulster Museum, Belfast.

19 Watts, W.W. *Geology for Beginners*. Macmillan, London, 3rd edition (1919), figure 112, p. 159.

20 Christen, S.M. *Rodolphe Christen: the story of an artist's life, 1859-1906*. Longmans, Green & Co., London (1910).

21 Lewis, C. *The Dating Game: one man's search for the age of the Earth*. Cambridge University Press (2000); Wyse Jackson, P.N. *The Chronologers' Quest: episodes in the search for the age of the Earth*. Cambridge University Press (2006).

22 Burek, C.V. 'The role of women in higher education – Bedford College and Newnham College', *The role of women in the history of geology*, edited by C.V. Burek and B. Higgs, 9-38.

Geological Society, London, Special Publications **281** (2007).

23 See account of this period of her life in Lewis, C. *op. cit.*

24 Wyse Jackson, P.N. 'Statistical Survey of Geological and Geomorphological Excursions undertaken by the Dublin Naturalists' Field Club 1886-1986', *Dublin Naturalists' Field Club Occasional Publication* **4** (1987), 1-14.

25 Wyse Jackson, P.N. 'Veronica Burns 1914-1998, Curator Geological Museum, Trinity College, Dublin 1964-1980', *The Geological Curator* **6** (1998), 339-340; Wyse Jackson, P.N. 'Veronica Conroy Burns (1914-1998)', *Irish Naturalists' Journal* **26** (1998), 1-4.

26 Wyse Jackson, *ibid.*, p. 339.

27 A photograph of the original committee, which includes Veronica, is reproduced on the cover of *Orbit*, the journal of the Irish Astronomical Society, for November 1987 (Volume 26, Number 2).

28 This is now in the Geological Museum, TCD.

29 Hudson, R.G.S., Clarke, M.J. & Sevastopulo, G.D. 'A detailed account of the fauna and age of a Waulsortian knoll reef limestone and associated shales, Feltrim, Co. Dublin, Ireland', *Scientific Transactions of the Royal Dublin Society* **2** (A) (1966), 251-272.

5. The Fabulous Boole Sisters, pp 60-71

Some publications by the Boole sisters:

Alicia Boole Stott:

Boole Stott, A. and P.H. Schoute 'On the sections of a block of eight cells by a space rotating about a plane', *Verhandlingen der Koninklijke van Wetenschappen te Amsterdam*, vol. 9 (1908), nr 7, 3-25.

Boole Stott, A. and P.H Schoute. 'Over wederkeerigheid in verband met halfregmatige polytopen en netter', *Verslagen der zittinger van de Wiskunde en Natuurkundige Afdeeling der Koninklijke Akademie van Wetenschappen*, vol. 19 (1910), 373-375.

Boole Stott, A. and P.H Schoute. 'Geometrical Deduction of Semi-regular from Regular Polytopes and Space Fillings', *Verhandlingen der Koninklijke van Wetenschappen te Amsterdam*, vol 11 (1910), nr. 1, 3-24

E.L.V. (Ethel Lilian Voynich, formerly Ethel Lilian Boole)

Stories from Garshin. London (1893); *Nihilism as it is*, translated by E.L. Voynich, London (1894); *The Humour of Russia*, Walter Scott, London (1895); *The Gadfly*, Heinemann, New York (1897); *Jack Raymond*, Heinemann, London (1901); *Olive Latham*, Heinemann, London (1904); *An interrupted Friendship* (1910); *Chopin's Letters*, New York (1931); *Put off thy shoes*, Heinemann, London (1946).

References

Blevins, Pamela, *Ethel Voynich – E.L.V. Revolutionary, Novelist, Translator, Composer*. www.musicweb-international.com/classrev/2005/Feb05/Voynich.htm. A non-subscription website. (accessed August 19, 2007).

Coey J.M.D. *George Francis FitzGerald*, Millenium Discourse. Available at www.tcd.ie/Physics/history/fitzgerald (accessed August 19, 2007).

MacTutor. A history of mathematics archive, hosted by St Andrews University, Scotland, and maintained by John J O'Connor and Edmund K Robertson. Includes brief biographies of George Boole and Alicia Boole Stott. www-history.mcs.st-andrews.ac.uk/ (accessed August 19, 2007)

MacHale, Desmond, *George Boole – his life and work,* Boole Press Dublin, 1985

Polo-Blanco Irene, *Theory and History of geometric models*, Academic Press, Europe, 2007 (doctoral dissertation, University of Groeningen, http://irs.ub.rug.nl/ppn/302252487) (accessed August 19, 2007).

Phillips, Tony, *The Princess of Polytopia: Alicia Boole Stott and the 120-cell.* American Mathematical Society online feature. http://www.ams.org/featurecolumn/archive/boole.html (accessed August 19, 2007).

Further sources: The Boole papers in UCC (1846-1910), Collection BP/1/. The three boxes include material pertaining to George Boole's wife Mary and their five daughters.

6. Torch-bearing Women Astronomers, pp 72–85

For Annie Maunder see also:

Brück, M.T. *Stars and Satellites: women in early astronomy in Britain and Ireland.* Springer 2009 (in press)

Ogilvie, Marilyn Bailey. 'Obligatory Amateurs: Annie Maunder (1868-1947) and British women astronomers at the dawn of professional astronomy', *British Journal for the History of Science* 33 (2000), 67-84

Wei Hock Soon, Willie and Yaskell, Steven H. *The Maunder Minimum and the Variable Sun-Earth Connection,* World Scientific, Singapore (2004)

Entry on Annie S.D. Maunder in the *New Oxford Dictionary of National Biography*, Oxford University Press (2003)

For Alice Everett see also:

Brück, M.T. 'Lady Computers at Greenwich in the early 1890s', *Quarterly Journal of the Royal Astronomical Society* vol 36, 1995

Creese, Mary R.S. *Ladies in the Laboratory?* Lanham Md and London (1998)

1 Brück, M.T. 'Alice Everett and Annie Russell Maunder, torch bearing women astronomers', *Irish Astronomical Journal* 21 (1994) 280-291

2 Brück, M.T. and Grew, S. 'The family background of Annie S.D.Maunder (née Russell)', *Irish Astronomical Journal* 23 (1996) 55-56

3 Brück, M.T. 'Lady Computers at Greenwich in the early 1890s', *Quarterly Journal of the Royal Astronomical Society* 36 (1995) 83-95

4 Maunder, E.W. *The Indian Eclipse 1898,* Hazel, Watson and Viney, London (1898).

5 Reproduced in the official Report on eclipses, *Memoirs of the Royal Astronomical Society* 64 (1925-29) and in the Maunders' book (reference 9 below)

6 Maunder, Annie. Letter to a friend to whom she gave the diagram in 1940. Archives of the

High Altitude Observatory, Boulder, Colorado. Courtesy Dr T. Bogdan.

7   For example in H.W.Newton, *The Face of the Sun*, pp51-52, Penguin Books (1958). Newton was a successor of Maunder as head of the solar department at Greenwich.

8   Willie Wei-Hock Soon and Steven H Yaskell. *The Maunder Minimum and the Variable Sun-Earth Connection*. Singapore: World Scientific (2004)

9   Maunder, A.S.D. 'Catalogue of recurrent groups of Sun Spots 1874-1906', Appendix to *Greenwich Observations 1907*. HM Stationery Office, Edinburgh (1909)

10 Maunder, A.S.D. 'The highways and the waterways of Mars', *Knowledge* 4 (1907), 167-171

11 Maunder, Annie S.D. and Maunder, E.Walter. *The Heavens and their Story*, Charles H. Kelly, London (1910)

12 Brück, M.T. *Agnes Mary Clerke and the rise of Astrophysics*, Chapter 13. Cambridge University Press (2002)

13 Ogilvie, Marilyn Bailey, 'Obligatory amateurs: Annie Maunder (1868-1947) and British women astronomers at the dawn of professional astronomy', *British Journal of the History of Science* (2000) **33**, 67-84.

14 Maunder, A.S.D. 'On Astronomical Allusions in Sacred Books of the East' *Journal of the Transactions of the Victoria Institute* 47 (1915), 181-232

15 Maunder, A.S.D. 'The origin of the constellations', *Observatory* 59 (1936), 367-375

16 Maunder, A.S.D. 'Reminiscences of the British Astronomical Association', *Journal of the British Astronomical Association* 42 (1943).

17 Moody T.W. and J.C. Beckett. *Queen's Belfast, 1845–1949: the history of a university,* Faber, London (1959)

18 Everett, A. 'Photographic magnitude of Nova Aurigae', *Journal of the British Astronomical Association* 2 (1892), p276 and other short contributions to the same journal.

19 Everett, A. 'Binary star orbits', *Monthly Notices of the Royal astronomical Society* 55 (1895) and 56 (1896)

20 Whitney, M.W and Everett, A. 'Observations of minor planets and a comet', *Astrophysical Journal* 20 (1900) (2 papers)

21 Watson, Katherine D., in: James, Frank, A.J. *The Common Purposes of Life, Science and Socety at the Royal Institution of Great Britain,* Ashgate, Aldershot (2002), Chapter 9.

22 Heinrich Hoverstadt. *Jena Glass and its scientific and industrial Applications*, translated and edited by J.D. Everett MA FRS and Alice Everett MA, London (1902)

23 Everett, A . Seven papers published 1919-24 in *Philosophical Magazine, Transactions of the Optical Society and Proceedings of the Physical Society* are listed in the Annual Reports of the National Physical Laboratory.

24 Everett, A. M.A. 'A More Compact Mirror Drum?' *Television*, February 1933; 'Mirror Drums and Metallic Reflection', *Television*, April 1933.

7. Revolutionary Doctors, pp 86-101

The author is grateful to: the National Library of Ireland for permission to quote from documents held in the collections: (1) MS 15344 NLI Dr Dorothy Price papers: history of Sinn Féin movement in W Cork, 1915-1918; and (2) Manuscript 6063, handwritten diary of Dorothy Price, April and May 1916, National Library of Ireland; and to the manuscripts department of Trinity College Library, Dublin for permission to quote from material in the Dorothy Price papers (TCD MS 7534/5; TCD MS 7534/18/1; TCD MS 7534/154/2).

1   Ó hÓgartaigh, Margaret, *Kathleen Lynn (Irishwoman, patriot, doctor)*, p1-2. Irish Academic Press, Dublin, 2006

2   Lynn diary, transcribed by Margaret Connolly, Royal College of Physicians of Ireland library, Kildare Street, Dublin

3   Cowell, John, *A Noontide Blazing, Brigid Lyons Thornton (rebel, soldier, doctor)*, Currach Press, Dublin, 2005

4   Manuscript 6063, handwritten diary of Dorothy Price, April and May 1916, National Library of Ireland

5   Smyth Hazel P, Kathleen Lynn, M.D, FRCSI (1874-1955), *Dublin Historical record*, Vol 30, 1977, cutting in Kirkpatrick Archive, Royal College of Physicians of Ireland, Kildare Street, Dublin

6   Ó Broin, Leon, *Protestant Nationalists in Northern Ireland, the Stopford connection*, p1-56. Gill and Macmillan, Dublin and New Jersey, 1985

7   McCoole Sinead, *No Ordinary Women, Irish Female Activists in the Revolutionary Years 1900-1923*, O'Brien Press, Dublin, 2003

8   St Ultan's minutebooks, Royal College of Physicians of Ireland, Kildare Street, Dublin

9   Hart, Peter, *The IRA and its enemies: violence and community in Cork 1916-1923* (Oxford, 1998), vii.

10 MS 15344 NLI Dr Dorothy Price papers: history of Sinn Fein movement in W Cork, 1915-1918

11 Hill, Myrtle. *Women in Ireland, a Century of Change* (Belfast, 2003), 80.

12 Finn, Irene, 'Women in the medical profession in Ireland 1876-1919', in: *Women and Paid Work in Ireland 1500-1930*, ed. Bernadette Whelan, Four Courts Press, Dublin 2000.

13 Mulholland Marie, *The politics and relationships of Kathleen Lynn*, p16-18. The Woodfield Press, Dublin 2002

14 Jones, Greta, *Captain of all these men of death. The history of tuberculosis in 19th and 20th century Ireland*, p 29. (New York, 2001)

15 Deeny James, *To Cure and to Care* (Dublin, 1989); Noel Browne, *Against the tide* (Dublin, 1986); John Horgan *Noel Browne, passionate outsider*, Gill & Macmillan Ltd, 2000.

16 Dorothy Stopford Price papers, TCD Manuscipts 7534, 152-4

17 Gerard R. Mandell, Douglas Raphael and John E. Bennett, *Principles and practices of infectious diseases* (Philadelphia, 2000), 166.

18 Dorothy Stopford Price, *Tuberculosis in childhood*; with a chapter on tuberculous orothopaedic lesions and other contributions by Henry F MacAuley. Imprint Bristol: J Wright; London, Simpkin Marshall, 1942, reprinted 1948.

19 Price papers, TCD, 7534, 7535

20 Ó hÓgartaigh Margaret, *Dr Dorothy Price and the elimination of Childhood Tuberculosis, in Ireland in the 1930s*, ed Augusteijn Joost, Four Courts Press, Dublin, 1999

21 Price, Liam, *Dr Dorothy Price – an account of twenty years fight against tuberculosis in Ireland*, printed at Univesity Press, Oxford, for private circulation only (1957). Copies available in UCD and RIA libraries.

8. Anatomy of a Bog Body, pp 102-113

Máire Delaney's key publications:

Bermingham Nóra and Delaney, M. *The bog body from Tumbeagh*, Wordwell, Ireland (2006)

Bermingham N and Delaney M, 'The Tumbeagh Bog Body', in *Institute of Field Archaeologists: yearbook and directory of members*, 2000, 40-2.

Delaney, M, Ó Floinn, R and Heckett E, 'Bog Body from Clongownagh, Baronstown West, County Kildare, Ireland', in B. Colges, J. Coles and M. Shou Jorgensen (eds), *Bog Bodies, Sacred sites and wetland archaeology*, 67-8. Wetland Archaeology Research Project Occasional paper 12. Exeter (1999)

Delaney, M, and Ó Floinn, R, 'A bog body from Meenybradden Bog, County Donegal, Ireland', In R.C. Turner and R.G. Scaife (eds.), *Bog Bodies: new discoveries and perspectives*, pp 123-32, London (1995)

Documentaries: Máire Delaney participated in two documentary programmes:

The 'Lady of the Sands' episode of the BBC television series 'Meet the Ancestors' - first broadcast on 15/01/1998. http://www.imdb.com/title/tt0273370/episodes#season-1

Discovery Channel 'Mummies Trilogy: Bog Bodies (2003)'; it can be downloaded for a nominal fee from: http://www.firstscience.tv/component/option,com_science/task,view/id,84/Itemid,18/

Some other sources consulted:

Science **277**. no. 5334, p1929 (1997)

'Bog finds call for new view of our Iron Age ancestors' report by Dick Ahlstrom, *The Irish Times*, January 7, 2006

Excavations.ie, database of Irish excavation reports, Clare 1971:10, Inishcaltra, R698850; and Clare 1973: 00006, Inishcaltra, R698850

Glob, P.V. *The Bog People*, Faber and Faber, London (1997)

'Kingship and sacrifice: Iron Age bog bodies and boundaries', *Archaeology Ireland*, Heritage Guide No. 35, September 2006

Keimelia: studies in medieval archaeology and history in memory of Tom Delaney, Gearoid Mac Niocaill and Patrick F Wallace eds., Galway University Press (1988)

Turner, R. C. 'The Lindow Man Phenomenon: ancient and modern', in: *Bog Bodies new Discoveries and Perspectives*, R.C. Turner & R.G. Scaife, eds., British Museum Press, (1995)

Turner RC and Scaife RG eds., *Bog bodies: new discoveries and perspectives*, British Museum Press (1995)

9. An Inspiring Zoologist, pp 114-123

Bibliography of chironomid papers by C.F. Humphries:

Humphries, C.F. (1936) 'An investigation of the profundal and sublittoral fauna of Windermere', *J. Anim. Ecol.* **5**: 29-52.

Humphries, C.F. (1937) Neue *Trichocladius*-Arten. *Stettin. ent. Ztg.* **98**: 185-195.

Humphries, C.F. (1938) 'The chironomid fauna of the Grosser Plöner See, the relative density of its members and their emergene period', *Arch. Hydrobiol.* **33**: 535-584.

Humphries, C.F. (1951) 'Metamorphosis of the Chironomidae. II. A description of the imago, larva and pupa of *Trichocladuis arduus*, n. sp., Goetghebuer and of the larva and pupa of *Trichocladius trifascia*, Edwards', *Hydrobiologia* **3**: 209-216.

Humphries, C.F. and W.E. Frost, (1937) 'River Liffey survey. The chironomid fauna of the submerged mosses', *Proc. R. Ir. Acad.* **43B**: 161-181.

Goetghebuer, M., C.F. Humphries, and Fitzgerald A.M. (1949) 'Metamorphosis of the Chironomidae. I. A description of the larvae, pupae and imagines of some members of the genus *Eukiefferiella* (Kieff.); of the larva of *Orthocladius crassicornis* (Goetgh.) and of the imago of *Orthocladius flaveolus* (Goetgh.)', *Hydrobiologia* **1**: 410-424.

10. Queen of the Plant Viruses, pp 124-133

Dr Phyllis Clinch published at least 26 scientific papers, 13 of them in the *Scientific Proceedings of the RDS*. Some of the more significant ones are:

(with J. Doyle), The Pentosan theory of cold resistance applied to conifers, *Scientific Proceedings of the RDS* **18**: 219-235, 1926

(with J. Doyle), Seasonal changes in conifer leaves, with special reference to enzymes and starch production, *Proc. Roy. Irish Acad.*, **37**: 373-414, 1927

Cytological studies of potato plants affected with certain virus diseases, *Sci Proc RDS* **20**: 143-172, 1932

(with JB Loughnane), Composition of interveinal mosaic of potatoes, *Nature* **135**: 883, 1935

(with J.B. Loughnane and P.A. Murphy), A study of the infiltration of viruses into seed potato stocks in the field, *Sci Proc RDS* **22**: 17-31, 1938

Virus diseases of tomato, *Éire Journal Dept of Agric* **38**: 24-47, 1941

(with J.B. Loughnane), Seed transmission of virus yellows of sugar beet (*Beta vulgaris* L) and the existence of strains of this virus in Éire, *Sci Proc RDS* **24**: 307-318, 1948

Award of the Boyle Medal, *Sci Proc RDS* **1**: 211-214, 1961

Ed. with R Charles Mollan, *A Profit and Loss Account of Science in Ireland*, Royal Dublin Society, 1983

11. The Doyenne of Irish Chemistry, pp 134-143

Key publications by Eva M Philbin

Prof Eva Philbin published 86 scientific papers, some of the more significant being:

'Studies in the Baker-Venkataraman transformation. The Auwers synthesis of 2-acylcoumaran-3-ones', *J. Chem. Soc.* 1954, 4174 (with W.I.A. O'Sullivan and T.S. Wheeler)

'Rearrangement in the demethylation of 2'-methoxyflavones. Part II: Further experiments and the determination of the composition of lotoflavin', *J. Chem Soc.* 1955, 4249 (with M.L. Doporto, K.M. Gallagher, J.E. Gowan, A.C. Hughes, T. Swain and T.S. Wheeler)

'Wesely-Moser rearrangement of chromonols and flavonols', *J. Chem. Soc.* 1956 4409 (with D.M.X. Donnelly and T.S. Wheeler)

'Studies in the chemistry of flavonoid epoxides: chemistry of natural and synthetic colouring matters and related fields', 1962, 167 (with T.S. Wheeler)

'Oxidation of chalcones (AFO reaction)', *Tetrahedron* 1963, **19**, 499 (with B.Cummins, D.M.X. Donnelly, J.F. Eades, H. Fletcher, J. Swirski, R.K.Wilson and T.S. Wheeler)

'Flavonoid epoxides VI stereochemistry of flavindogenide epoxides', *Tetrahedron* 1970, **26**, 2533 (with D.D. Keane and W.I O'Sullivan)

'Steric and electronic effects in the Emilewicz Von Kostanecki cyclisation of chalcone dihalides', *Proc Royal Irish Acad.* 1983 **83B** 49 (with J.A. Donnelly, J.P.Acton and Dorothy J. Donnelly).

'Richard Kirwan, a Galway scientist 1733-1812', by Eva M.Philbin, in: *Galway Town and Gown 1484-1984* pp110-126 (ed. Diarmuid Ó Cearbhaill)

'Chemistry' by Eva M. Philbin, in: *Royal Irish Academy a bicentennial History 1785-1985*, RIA (1985) pp 274-300.

12. The Stuff of Diamonds, pp 144-155

1   Hodgkin, Dorothy M.C., 'Kathleen Londsdale. 28 January 1903-1 April 1971'. *Biographical Memoirs of Fellows of the Royal Society*, vol 21 (Nov 1975), p 447. This 37-page memoir, written by Lonsdale's friend and colleague, provides personal and professional insights that will delight anyone wishing to read more about Kathleen Lonsdale. It contains a comprehensive list of Lonsdale's publications, honours, and conferences attended. This current account of Dame Lonsdale's life draws on Hodgkin's memoir extensively – future references in the text are not individually annotated.

2   http://nobelprize.org/nobel_prizes/physics/laureates/1915/wl-bragg-bio.html

3   Julian, M.M. 'Women in Crystallography' in *Women of Science* (Bloomington: Indiana University Press, 1990) 341.

4   University College London. Administrative/biographical history. Introduction to papers and correspondence of Dame Kathleen Lonsdale 1903-1971.
    www.archiveshub.ac.uk/news/03030502.html.

5   Lonsdale, Kathleen, 'Women Scientists – Why so Few?' *Laboratory Equipment Digest*, 1971, p85.

6   Fourier analysis, named after Joseph Fourier's introduction of the Fourier series, entails decomposing a function in terms of sinusoidal functions (basis functions) of various frequencies that can be recombined to obtain the original function.

7   Hodgkin, Dorothy. *Op.cit.*, p467.

8   Julian, M.M. *Op. cit.* p356.

9   Lonsdale, K, 'Human Stones', *Scientific American*, **219** (1968) 104-111.

10 The Pugwash Conferences on Science and World Affairs, awarded the 1995 Nobel Peace Prize, take their name from the location of the first 1957 meeting, held in Pugwash, Nova Scotia, Canada. There, the prime objectives established were: prevention of a nuclear war, and disarmament. Subsequent Pugwash meetings concentrated on reducing the danger of the nuclear arms race; calling for a total ban on the testing of nuclear weapons; seeking measures to limit the proliferation of nuclear weapons; and searching for means of defusing crises to prevent their escalation into nuclear conflict.

11 Lonsdale, Kathleen, Women in Science: Reminiscences and Reflections, *Impact of Science on Society* (1970) 20:45-49.

12 Lonsdale, Kathleen, Women in Science, *op. cit.*

13 Lonsdale, Kathleen, 'Science and the Good Life', *Presidential Address to the British Association for the Advancement of Science*, (1968). Published by the BAAS as an 11-page pamphlet.

14 Robertson, J.M., 'Kathleen Lonsdale', *Dictionary of Scientific Biography*, III, (New York, Scribners: (1973) 484-486

13. One of the World's First Computer Programmers, pp 156–167

1 An account of the first 'lady computers' employed at the Royal Observatory, Greenwich, in the 1890s is given by Máire Bruck, 'Bringing the heavens down to earth', in: *Stars, Shells and Bluebells*, WITS (1997) pp70-71. See also this volume, page xxx.

2 Shurkin, Joel. *Engines of the Mind: the Evolution of the Computer from Mainframes to Microprocessors.* Norton, New York (1996, 1984) pp126-7.

3 Barkley, Fritz, W. 'The Women of ENIAC'. *Annals of the History of Computing*, Vol 18 No 3 (1996) p 16.

4 Shurkin, Joel. *Op.cit.* p127.

5 Levy, Claudia. 'Betty Holberton Dies; Helped U.S. Develop Computer Languages'. *Washington Post*, 11 Dec 2001, p. B7.

6 Shurkin, Joel. *Op. Cit.* p188.

7 Kennedy, T.B Jr. 'Electrical Computer Flashes Answers, May Speed Engineering.' *New York Times* (Feb 15, 1946) p 1.

8 Sobel, Rachel K. 'Faulty Memory'. *US News & World Report*, Vol 132, No 4 (11 Feb 2002) p 70.

9 Mauchly, Kathleen R. 'John Mauchly's Early Years'. *Annals of the History of Computing*, Vol 6, No 2, (April 1984) pp 116-138.

10 Barkley, Fritz, W. *Op. cit.* p 27.

11 Petzinger, Tom. 'History of software begins with the work of some brainy women'. *Wall Street Journal* (November 1996).

12 Tanaka, Wendy. 'Philadelphia Developers of First Commercial Computer Honored, Reminisce'. *Philadelphia Inquirer* (June 21, 2001) p F03.

Additional image credits

WITS is indebted to the many people and institutions who provided illustrations for this volume.

We thank Dr Stan Solomon, Deputy Director of the High Altitude Observatory, National Center for Atmospheric Research, Boulder, Colorado, for assistance with sourcing the images of Maunder 'butterfly diagram' (page 79) and the drawing of the long coronal ray (page 77).

The photographs of Kay McNulty's high school graduation (page 158) and the differential analyzer, Moore School of Electrical Engineering (page 161) are files from the Wikimedia Commons http://en.wikipedia.org/wiki/Kathleen_Antonelli accessed December 1, 2008.

DISCLAIMER: every effort has been made to trace the copyright holders of the images reproduced in this publication. The publishers apologise if any image has inadvertently been reproduced without permission; to rectify this in future editions, we ask owners of copyright, not acknowledged here, to contact us.

Abbreviations

Some of the main abbreviations used in the text:

BAA   British Astronomical Association

BAAS British Association for the Advancement of Science

BNFC Belfast Naturalists' Field Club

DIAS Dublin Institute for Advanced Studies

DNFC Dublin Naturalists' Field Club

DSS   Dublin Statistical Society

GSI   Geological Survey of Ireland

NUI   National University of Ireland

QUB   Queen's University, Belfast

RDS   Royal Dublin Society

RUI   Royal University of Ireland

TCD   Trinity College, Dublin

UCG   University College Galway

Index

Principal people and institutions mentioned in the text, bold indicates a main entry.

WITS

women in technology
and science

Get your WITS about you!

Membership is open to women and men throughout Ireland who work, have worked or are studying in any area of science, engineering or technology

---

Membership Type

a) New Member ☐   b) Renewal for 2009 ☐

Membership Fees

Individual €50 ☐   Concessions €20 (retired, unemployed and student members) ☐

Receipt Required: Y ☐   N ☐

Membership Details

Title (Dr, Ms, Mr, Mrs) ....

Surname: .... First Name: ....

Job/Dept (optional): ....

Address: ....

....

Contact telephone(s): home .... work .... mobile ....

Email Address (s) 1. ....

2. ....

For Office Use Only
Cash/Cheque/PO Received ☐   Date: _____   Processed by: _____

Complete this form and send it, with your subscription, to:
WITS, PO Box 3783, Dublin 4, Ireland
E-mail : wits@iol.ie   Web: www.witsireland.com

Note: WITS sends most communication to members electronically for cost reasons. Membership information will be stored electronically by WITS for administration and circulation purposes, but will not be disclosed or circulated, in accordance with Data Protection legislation.